TRIBES AND CASTES OF RAJASTHAN

TRIBES AND CASTES OF RAJASTHAN

M. A. SHERRING

GYAN

Published by

Gyan Publishing House
5, Ansari Road
Daryaganj, New Delhi-110002
Phone: 011-47034999, 9811692060
E-mail: books@gyanbooks.com

Distribution Network
gyanbooks.com
India, USA, Canada, UK, Australia

ISBN: 978-93-7097-059-5 (PB)

First Published, 1918

2nd Impression 2025

Printed at: Gyan Press, Delhi.

TRIBES AND CASTES OF RAJASTHAN
Author: M. A. SHERRING

THE
TRIBES AND CASTES
OF RAJASTHAN

THE TRIBES AND CASTES OF RAJASTHAN

TOGETHER WITH
DESCRIPTION OF SACRED AND CELEBRATED
PLACES OF HISTORICAL VALUE
OF RAJASTHAN

BY
M. A. SHERRING, M.A., LL.B.

1975

PREFACE.

THIS volume was left by the late Mr. Sherring in a complete state, and was placed in our hands shortly after his death. It has not had the benefit of the Author's revision in passing through the Press; but the want of it is the less to be deplored, as it was Mr. Sherring's habitual practice to make his manuscript quite perfect before entrusting it to Printers; and we therefore feel confident that no material errors can have crept in.

The Index to the first and second volumes was made by Mr. Sherring; the Index to the third volume has been incorporated on the same plan.

Mr. Sherring contemplated a Map showing the location of the various castes, which would have added greatly to the value of the work; but we regret it was impossible, without his participation, to prepare one.

THE PUBLISHERS.

List of Books, Reports, Records, and other Documents, quoted or referred to in the third volume of "Hindu Tribes and Castes."

Extract from the General Memoir of the Survey of Travancore. By Lieutenant P. E. Conner, Madras Journal of Literature and Science. for October, 1833, and January, 1834.

Geographical and Statistical Memoir of a Survey of the Neilgherry Mountains, under the superintendence of Captain J. Ochterlony, 1847. Madras Journal of Literature, Vol. XV.

Descriptive Sketch of the various Tribes and Castes of Mysore. By Mr. S. B. Kristnasawmy Iyengar.

The Land of Charity—A Descriptive Account of Travancore and its People. By the Rev. Samuel Mateer, F. L. S.

Tribes of South India. By the Rev. J. F. Kearns, Missionary of the Society for the Propagation of the Gospel, Tinnevelly.

Description of the Administrative System of Travancore. By V. Kristno Row, late Dewan of Travancore. Edited by Major Drury, at the request of F. N. Maltby, Esq., Resident at the Courts of Travancore and Cochin.

The Aboriginal Tribes of the Neilgherry Hills. By Lieut.-Colonel W. Ross King.

The Native States of India. By Colonel Malleson.

Report on the Census of the Madras Presidency for 1871. By Surgeon-Major W. R. Cornish, Sanitary Commissioner for Madras.

The Tribes inhabiting the Neilgherry Hills. By the Rev. F. Metz, Missionary of the Basle Missionary Society.

A Phrenologist among the Todas. By Lieut.-Colonel W. E. Marshall, Bengal Staff Corps.

Manual of Vizagapatam. By Mr. D. F. Carmichael, Magistrate, and Agent of the Governor of Fort St. George.

The Madura Country. A Manual compiled by order of the Madras Government, by J. H. Nelson, Esq., M.A., Madras Civil Service.

Transactions of the Ethnological Society, New Series, Vol. III, Article on some rude Tribes of Southern India. By Dr. Shortt.

Manual of the Nellore District in the Presidency of Madras. By John A. C. Boswell, Esq., M. C. S., Collector and Magistrate of the Kistna District.

Gazetteer of Ajmere-Merwara. By Mr. J. D. Latouche, B. C. S.

Gazetteer of the Bikaneer State. By Captain Powlett, Political Agent, Ulwar.

Gazetteer of the Karauli State. By Captain Powlett.

Gazetteer of Marwar. By Major C. K. M. Walter, Political Agent, Marwar.

Gazetteer of Mattani. By Major Walter.

Gazetteer of Jeysalmere. By Major Walter.

Gazetteer of Rajputana, 1st and 2nd Volumes.

History of Mewar. By Captain J. C. Brookes.

Gazetteer of Southern India. By Messrs. Pharoah & Co, Madras.

Essay on the Creed, Customs, and Literature of the Jangams. By Charles P. Brown, Esq., Madras Civil Service.

Grammar of the Dravidian Languages. By the Rev. Dr. Caldwell. Second Edition.

Manual of the District of Cuddapah. By J. D. B. Gribble, Esq., M. C. S., Sub-Collector of the Cuddapah District.

Hindu Tribes and Castes, Vols. I and II. By the Rev. M. A. Sherring.

The Tinnevelly Shanars. By Bishop Caldwell.

Mysore and Coorg. A Gazetteer compiled by the Government of India, by Mr. Lewis Rice, Director of Public Instruction, Mysore and Coorg. Vols. I and II.

The Indian Antiquary, Vol. V, p. 354. Extract from the work of Von Philipp Van Mokern, entitled 'Ostindien seine Geshichte, Cultur, und seine Bewohner.'

Indian Caste. By the late Rev. Dr. Wilson, F. R. S., Missionary of the Free Church of Scotland, Bombay. 2 Vols.

Manual of the South Arcot District. By J. H. Garstin, M. C. S., Collector of South Arcot.

The Chiefs of Central India. By G. R. Aberigh-Mackay. Vol. I.

CONTENTS.

PART I.—THE TRIBES AND CASTES OF RAJPUTANA.

CHAPTER I.

The Tribes and Castes of Rajputana.

CHAPTER II.

The Brahmanical Tribes.

CHAPTER III.

The Rajpoot Tribes.

CHAPTER IV.

The Rajpoot Tribes—*(Continued.)*

CHAPTER V.

Castes.

CHAPTER VI.

The Mair, or Mar Tribes.

CHAPTER VII.

CHAPTER VIII.

The Mahomedan Tribes.

PART II.—THE TRIBES AND CASTES OF THE MADRAS PRESIDENCY.

CHAPTER I.

SECTION I.—THE BRAHMANICAL CASTES.

SECTION II.—THE KSHATRIYA, KETHREE, OR RAJPOOT TRIBES.

SECTION III.—THE VAISYA CASTES—CHETTIES OR SETTIES.

CHAPTER II.

SECTION I.—THE AGRICULTURAL TRIBES—VELLALARS.

SECTION II.—THE AGRICULTURAL LABOURING TRIBES.

CHAPTER III.

2

CHAPTER IV.

Aboriginal and Low-caste Tribes.

CHAPTER V.

Aboriginal and Low-caste Tribes.—*(Continued.)*

CHAPTER VI.

Tribes and Castes of Mysore.

CHAPTER VII.

Tribes of the Neilgherry Hills.

CHAPTER VIII.

Tribes and Castes of Travancore and Tinnevelly.

SECTION I.—TRIBES OF TRAVANCORE.

SECTION II.—TRIBES OF TINNEVELLY.

CHAPTER IX.

Page.

CHAPTER X.

PART III.—DISSERTATIONS ON

PART I.

THE TRIBES AND CASTES

OF

RAJPUTANA.

CHAPTER I.

THE TRIBES AND CASTES OF RAJPUTANA.

DISTRIBUTION OF THE RULING RAJPOOT TRIBES AMONG THE RAJPOOT STATES. NATURE OF THE GOVERNMENT OF A RAJPOOT CHIEF. THE AGRICULTURAL CLASSES. BHUMIA TENURES. THE CUSTOM OF GAVELKIND. THE WORSHIP OF THE SNAKE. SACRED AND CELEBRATED PLACES IN RAJPUTANA:—THE PUSHKAR LAKE; THE DARGAH AT AJMERE; THE GREAT MOSQUE AT AJMERE; THE TEMPLE AND MONASTERY OF DADU PANTH AT BARAHNA, NEAR THE SAMBHAR LAKE; THE OLD ROYAL PALACE AT AMBER, IN JEYPORE; THE GUTTA; THE OBSERVATORY AT JEYPORE; THE SILLA DEVI TEMPLE; THE AMBER-KISWAS SHRINE; THE MONASTERY AND SHRINES OF THE DADU PANTHIS AT NARAINA; THE TRIPOLIA; JAIN TEMPLES AT SANGARER; THE CHARAN-PADH; THE SHRINES AT BAIRAT; THE JAIN TEMPLE AT LADORVA; THE ANCIENT JAIN TEMPLES OF JESALMERE; THE MAHA SUTTEE AT BUNDEE. MARRIAGE CUSTOMS IN RAJPUTANA.

The country of Rajputana possesses an area of about hundred and thirty thousand square miles, separated into the following nineteen States, namely:—Banswara, Bhurtpore, Bikaneer, Bundee, Dholpore, Dungarpore, Jeypore, Jesalmere, Jhalawar, Karauli, Kishengarh, Kotah, Marwar, Meywar, Pertabgarh, Sirdhee, Tonk, Ulwar, and Ajmere-Merwara. With the exception of Ajmere, which is a British province, all the remaining States are independent and have their own ruling chiefs, who are, however, more or less controlled by the British Government through its Political Agents. Tonk is governed by a Mahomedan prince, Bhurtpore and Dholpore by Jâts, and the remaining fifteen States by Rajpoot chiefs. There is also a sixteenth Rajpoot State, that of Shahpore, which is of small extent, and has no treaty with the empire.

At what date Rajpoots first entered Rajputana is unknown. There is reason to believe that, at one time, the great Râthor kingdom of Kanouj once included a portion of this tract; and it is quite certain that, at the period of the commencement of the Mahomedan rule in India, the Chauhâns were in Ajmere, the Râthors were in Kanouj, the Solankhis were in Gujerat, the Gâhlots were in Meywar, the Râthors and Sodas were in the barren deserts of the north-west, and the Kachwahas were in Jeypore. When the Mahomedans entered India, Rajpoot kings were ruling over extensive tracts, extending from the Punjab to Ajudhiya, the ancient term for Oudh. Had these monarchs and their tribes united together firmly, and placed themselves under one or two sagacious commanders, they would have stemmed the tide of Mahomedan invaders, and driven them back again beyond the Himalaya mountains. Unfortunately, they were at constant feud with one another, and hence, gradually, fell a prey to the sword of the conqueror. In the latter half of the twelfth century a fierce war broke out between the Solankhis of Anhalwara and the Chauhâns of Ajmere, and between the Chauhâns and the Râthors of Kanouj. Weakened by tribal strife, and before they had recovered themselves, these tribes were attacked by the Mahomedan invaders; and Shahabuddin, aided by his great lieutenant Kutbuddin, gained possession of Delhi, Ajmere, Kanouj, and Anhalwara.

The tribal wars of the great Rajpoot houses, and their eventual subjugation by a foreign foe, produced the separation and dispersion of the Rajpoot tribes, and led to their occupying, for the most part, new territories. The Bhâtis, after many vicissitudes, settled in Jesalmere, the Râthors in Marwar, the Sisodiyas in Meywar, and the Jâdons in the vicinity of the Chambal. These and other tribes have experienced various fortunes down to the present time, which would be better discussed in a history of Rajputana than in a work restricted to an account of the individual tribes and castes. One important event, however, in regard to these tribes must not be passed over. This is the growth of the Oodipore State in the sixteenth century and its predominance in Central India under its great chief, Rana Sanga, and the complete overthrow of this Prince, and of all the Rajpoot tribes attached to him, at the hands of Babar, in the famous battle of Futtehpore-Sikri, in the year 1527. In consequence of this serious defeat the Sisodiyas lost their supremacy, which passed over to the Râthors. But the Rajpoot tribes lost their independence. Moreover, some of the chiefs entered the service of the Mahomedan emperor, and some permitted their daughters to marry Mahomedan princes. Up to the time of Akbar, the Rajpoot chiefs, more or less, preserved their independence; but in a short time they lost this position and became simply feudatories of the emperor.

When Nadir Shah entered India, a compact was made between the three great tribes of the Sisodiyas, Râthors, and Kachwahas, which would have had an important result politically, had it not been for the haughty stipulation of the Sisodiyas that the sons of Râthor and Kachwaha chiefs by Sisodiya wives should take precedence of sons borne by wives of other tribes. The consequence was, that a feud arose, which broke up the compact. At the end of the last century

Rajputana fell almost completely under the sway of the Mahrattas, who 'exacted tribute, ransomed cities, annexed territory, and extorted subsidies.' Its oppressors were, for the most part, Sindia and Holkar. These potentates succumbed to the British army after severe fighting and various changes; but it was not until the years 1817 and 1818 that the Rajputana chiefs were finally taken under British protection, and firmly established in their territories again. The State of Bhurtpore was not settled till afterwards, and not indeed till a British force had stormed the city, which event took place in the month of January, 1825.

Eighteen of the Rajpoot States are of the first rank, and are under treaty with the British Government. Sixteen States, including Shahpore, are governed by Rajpoot chiefs of six tribes, namely, Râthor, Sisodiya, Chauhân, Jâdon, Kachwaha, and Jhâla, which are distributed as follows :—

Distribution of Rajpoot States among Rajpoot Tribes.

State.	Ruling Tribe.
Jodhpore (Marwar)	Râthor.
Bikaneer	Ditto.
Kishengarh	Ditto.
Meywar (Oodipore)	Sisodiya.
Banswara	Ditto.
Dungarpore	Ditto.
Pertabgarh	Ditto.
Shahpore	Ditto.
Bundee	Chauhân, of the Hâra branch.
Kotah	Ditto ditto.
Sirohee	Ditto, of the Deoria branch.
Karauli	Jâdon, of the Bhâti branch.
Jesalmere	Ditto ditto.
Jeypore	Kachwaha.
Ulwar	Ditto, of the Naruka branch.
Jhalawar	Jhâla (*a*).

In addition there are various chiefships not reckoned as States. One of these is Khetri, in the Shekhawatee District, which is held on a tenure similar to that of Shahpore. Beyond Bundee and Kotah, on the eastern side of Rajputana, are seven small tracts, called the seven Kotris, possessed by seven families

(*a*) The Rajputana Gazetteer, Vol. I. pp. 54-5.

of the Chauhân Hâra Rajpoots, under special compact with the British Government. Their chiefs are responsible to the head of the Hâra tribe. There are also the chiefs of Sikar in Jeypore, Nimrana in Ulwar, Fathgarh in Kishengarh, and Kusalgarh in Banswara. Then, too, there are the Bheel chiefs of the Meywar hill regions, and the Thakur of Lawa. Besides these minor chieftains there are others of a still lower rank, such as the Rao of Salumbar, in Meywar, a ruler of much influence in the Chappan.

Three Rajputana States are not governed by Rajpoot princes. One of these is Tonk, consisting of six separate districts, three of which only lie within the boundaries of Rajputana. They are ruled by a nawab, according to the convention made with Ameer Khan in 1817. The remaining,—namely, Bhurtpore and Dholpore,—are held by Jât chiefs. These States were not included within the treaties of 1817 and 1818, which were of so much importance to the consolidation of the other Rajputana States (*a*).

A Rajpoot chief rules as the head of a tribe divided into numerous clans, at the head of which are petty chiefs, generally members of his own family, all of whom acknowledge his sovereignty and pay him tribute, while his own authority is only absolute over those tracts which are not in their hands or under their control. The tenure differs in different States, but this is the general type which it assumes. The domestic and clannish character is seen more prominently in the western than in the eastern States of Rajputana. It will be obvious that this mode of tenure contributes greatly to the maintenance of an extensive Rajpoot aristocracy, and to the self-reliance, pride, and love of display, for which it is famous. Although the smaller chiefs are obliged to pay tribute and homage, and also to perform certain services to their paramount lord, nevertheless, their right to their estates and to lordship over them is indefeasible, and in some cases is as ancient as the right of the ruling prince to the State which he governs. The Thakurs, or great landholders, similarly claim from their dependants customary dues or services. The clannishness of the eastern States, as just remarked, is weaker than in the western. This arises from the fact that those provinces were much more accessible to Mahomedan and Mahratta invaders, and hence were brought much more under their influence than those further west. Moreover, the former contains a much small Rajpoot population than the latter. Zalim Singh well nigh ruined the clans of Kotah. The head of the Bundee State rules almost absolutely, for although in that province there are several persons, relatives of the Bundee Rajah, holding large estates, yet they have no separate jurisdiction.

(*a*) The Rajputana Gazetteer, Vol. I, p. 56.

In Bhurtpore and Dholpore, the power of the chief is supreme, as it is also for the most part in Tonk. The rule, however, is not without an exception, for Karauli, in the east, exhibits the clannish system to perfection.

The Rajpoot population, while considerable in some States, in no State outnumbers all the other classes put together. The Rajpoots, however, are everywhere first in rank and influence, and next to them come the Brahmans. The Chârans and Bhâts are genealogists and bards. The Jâts and Gûjars are agriculturists. The Meenas, Mers, and Meos were, probably, in closer alliance than they are now, and may have proceeded from the same original stock. Their traditions state that they have partly sprung from old Rajpoot tribes. Moreover, they are, to some extent, in intimate association with the Bheels. The Meos were formerly Hindus, but are now Mahomedans. Some of the Bheel tribes, those of purer blood, inhabit wild and desolate tracts, and are semi-independent. Other Bheels, a rude people, have intermingled with Hindus in their villages away from the civilization of the cities.

Respecting the geographical distribution of the principal Rajpoot tribes in Rajputana, the Râthors are most numerous in Marwar, Bikaneer, Jesalmere, Kishengarh, and the central tracts of Ajmere. Jesalmere is under the government of the Bhâtis. The Kachwahas predominate in Ulwar and Jeypore, while the territory in the north of Jeypore belongs to the Shekhawatis. The Chauhâns, especially the Hâra tribes, are strong in the eastern States. The Deorias, also Chauhâns, hold Sirohee. Nimrana is likewise in the hands of the Chauhâns, and so is Kusalgarh. The Sisodiyas are paramount in Meywar and the north-west States below the Arvalis, the head of the tribe being the Maharana of Oodipore. The Parihars, Pramaras, and Solankhis, once powerful tribes, are found in some of the States, but they are few in number, and without much influence (*a*).

These Rajpoots of Rajputana are not so rigidly attached to caste as their brethren in other parts, and are not very respectful to Brahmans. They eat animal food, especially the flesh of goats and wild pigs, drink the strongest spirits, consume opium inordinately, and are exceedingly superstitious, the poorer classes being profoundly ignorant. With the exception of the States of Mallani and Shekhawatee, the law of primogeniture prevails in all the States.

In some States the authority of the principal chief is of a very limited character. For example, the Thakurs, or great landholders, of Banswara, of all ranks, are said to possess full and entire jurisdiction within their several estates, and will neither allow their subjects (as they are termed) to be summoned to the

(*a*) The Rajputana Gazetteer, Vol. I, pp. 66, 67.

capital of the State, nor to be interfered with, or any way punished, by orders of the sovereign prince.

Mr. Abcrigh-Mackay, in his interesting book on the Chiefs of Central India, makes a significant and important statement respecting many of the great Rajpoot families at the present time. I shall quote his observations on this point: "The saddest thing in all Rajwarra at the present day," he remarks, "is the condition of the royal caste. The children of the sun and moon, the children of the fire-fountain, seem to have forgotten the inspiriting traditions of their race, and have sunk into a state of slothful ignorance and debauchery that mournfully contrast with the chivalrous heroism, the judicious and active patriotism, the refined culture, and the generous virtue of their ancestors. The memory of a hundred noble deeds that adorn their annals, is still fresh in the minds of all men; and the names of many Rajpoot princes, of comparatively recent times, will never die while a history of India remains. Rana Sanga of Mewar, enemy of the Moghul; Jai Singh Sewai, of Jeypore, scholar statesman, and soldier; Sur Singh, Gaj Singh, Jeswant Singh, the glorious paladins of Marwar,—these are surely names to conjure with—yet they would now seem to excite but little emulation in the breasts of many of those in whose veins their blood flows, and who still bear their undying names. Hardly able to read or write his own language—ignorant of all pertaining to his country, pertaining to his race, pertaining to his State, pertaining to his sacred office as a ruler of men—the petty Rajpoot of the present day often saunters away his miserable existence in the society of abominable creatures that cast discredit on the name of servant. Besotted with spirits and opium, dull, morose, and wretched, he knows nothing of his affairs; and leaves everything to plundering 'managers' and 'deputy managers.' He is generally hopelessly in debt. He seldom cares for any thing but the merest shadow of his dignity, the ceremony with which he is treated. Of this he is insanely jealous. That all the honours due to royalty and Rajpoot blood should be paid him; that he should be saluted with guns, and received at the edge of carpets, and followed by escorts of cavalry; that his daughters should be married at an early age to princes of higher clans than his own; that his Thakurs should attend him at the Dassehra, and perform the precise ritual of allegiance—all this is what he craves. It never occurs to him to consider whether he wears his princely honours worthily, and whether those who show him the outward observances of respect, love or honour him in their hearts. But there is reason to believe that a new generation of Rajpoot princes is springing up, who will add to the courtly manners of which the most degenerate Rajpoot is never destitute, a knowledge of affairs, a desire to govern well, and an enthusiasm for manly sports, the battles of peaceful days. They, however, will have much to do to restore the drooping prestige of the royal caste" (*a*).

The agricultural classes in Rajputana occupy a higher social status than they commonly do in the provinces of British India. They are a manly, independent race exhibiting a good deal of self-respect, and are treated with consideration by native chiefs. They will only perform agricultural duties, and regard themselves as much superior to day-labourers and menial servants, who, unlike the similar class under British rule, are a down-trodden, mean-spirited people.

Bhûmia Tenures.

There is a peculiar tenure prevalent among Rajpoots, known as Bhûm, which properly means the soil, by virtue of which the Bhûmia, or holder of land under this tenure, has a proprietorship very different from that of feudal chiefs and tenants of crown-lands. Originally, they seem to have belonged to the aristocratic class, but gradually sank from that position to that which they now occupy, which is, however, one of respectability and of considerable independence. They still pay a small quit-rent to their chief for their lands, but are otherwise left uncontrolled. This old form of the Bhûm tenure has assumed various phases, arising from changes in grants of land in addition to the original kind of tenure; yet they were alike in this, that an "hereditary, non-resumable, and inalienable property in the soil was inseparably bound up with a revenue-free title. Bhûm was given as compensation for bloodshed, in order to quell a feud—for distinguished services in the field—for protection of a border—or for watch and ward of a village" (*b*). In all cases the tenure is the same, and is very highly esteemed by Rajpoots of all classes, so that some chiefs of superior rank think it no dishonour to be styled Bhûmias. "The Maharaja of Kishengarh," says Mr. J. D. La Touche, "the Thakur of Fathgarh, the Thakur of Junia, the Thakur of Bandunwara, and the Thakur of Tantoti, are among the Bhûmias of Ajmere" (*c*). In this province there are no less than one hundred and nine tenures of this nature. It is somewhat singular that the old Rajpoot families, which formerly held rule in Ajmere as kings, should be so little represented in these Bhûmias. A few are in the hands of the Gaur Rajpoots, but the Chauhâns and Pramars seem to be entirely without any in their possession, while most of them, in fact nearly all, are held by Râthors.

(*a*) The Chiefs of Central India, by G. R. Aberigh-Mackay, Esq., Vol. I, pp. xxx, xxxi.
(*b*) The Rajputana Gazetteer, Vol. II, p. 30.
(*c*) *Ibid.*

Certain public duties were required of the Bhûmias, namely, to defend their own villages from robbers, to afford protection to travellers, and to compensate those who had through their misadvertence been plundered. This last condition is still carried out through the instrumentality of the International Court of Advocates. Thus, if a robbery has happened within the jurisdiction of any village, its head or chief is bound to make good the loss (*a*).

The Bhûmia chiefs of Ogna, Panurwa, Jowra, and Jowas, in the Meywar State, are partly of Bheel and partly of Rajpoot origin. They pay tribute to the Maharana. One or two of them, it is said, can muster a considerable body of men armed with bow and arrow.

The Custom of Gavelkind.

This custom, which has the force of law, prevails in Mallani, where it seems to have been productive of much disorder and strife. On the death of a father his property is equally divided among his sons. The land, therefore, has been divided and subdivided from generation to generation among a great number of claimants, so that it is split up into a multitude of proprietorships. Endless feuds arose in former times among families and clans from these minute divisions of estates, and, on account of the bloodshed which often occurred, the Jodhpore chiefs at length interfered, and eventually asserted a right of sovereignty over the whole province (*b*).

The Worship of the Snake.

Every village in the State of Mallani has a sacred slab with the figure of a serpent sculptured upon it, which is an object of devout veneration by all the inhabitants. The slab is placed in a prominent position under a tree, generally the *khejra*, and is especially resorted to by anyone who has been stung by a snake (*c*).

SACRED AND CELEBRATED PLACES IN RAJPUTANA.

The Pushkar Lake.

This is a spot of great sanctity in the estimation of Hindus for two reasons,—the first of which is, that Brahmâ is supposed to have performed a great religious ceremony; and the second, that the formerly famous and now extinct River Sâras-

(*a*) The Rajputana Gazetteer. Vol. II, p. 30.
(*b*) *Ibid*, p. 266.
(*c*) *Ibid*, p. 282.

wati is believed to reappear in this lake, not in one stream, but in five,—namely, the Suprabha, flowing into Jyesht Pushkar; the Sudha, which enters the Madhya Pushkar; the Kanka, falling into Kamsht Pushkar; and the Nanda, flowing past Nand; and the Prâchi, flowing by Hakran. No other lake bears so sacred a character as the Pushkar Lake, with the single exception of the Manusarowar Lake in Thibet. An account of the legends connected with it is found in the Pushkar Mahâtam of the Padma Purâna. So many Hindus are said to have bathed in the lake after Brahmâ had performed the ceremony, and to have gone to heaven in consequence, that it became inconveniently crowded; and therefore Brahmâ, to remedy the difficulty and to stay the influx of saints into heaven, abolished the sanctity of the Pushkar Lake, except during the days intervening between the eleventh day of the month of Kartik and the full-moon next succeeding. From this, or from other reasons, the sacred virtues of the lake were lost sight of, until they were re-discovered by Rajah Nahar Rao Parihâr, who was cured of a skin disease by bathing in its waters. He, in gratitude, built several ghâts on the banks of the lake, and had it newly excavated and thereby cleansed. There are five important temples in Pushkar, of comparatively modern date, erected to Brahmâ, Savitri, Badri Narayana, Vârâha, and Shiva Atmateswara. The ancient temples formerly here were destroyed by the Moghal emperors, especially Aurungzebe, who raised a mosque on the site of a temple dedicated to Keshu Rae. The mosque is still standing. It is worthy of remark that the temple to Brahmâ is the only one in all India consecrated to the worship of that deity, who, although regarded by Hindus as the creator, is nevertheless one of the most unpopular of Hindu divinities. The reason of his unpopularity is well-known, and arises from gross licentiousness, of which, according to tradition, Brahmâ was once guilty.

The fish of the lake, and the wild fowl floating upon its surface, together with all animals within certain limits of the lake, are protected by ancient charters. As animal life is sacred to the religious Hindu, it is a crime to take the life of any creature either within the lake or in its neighbourhood. Not long since the entire population around the lake was greatly excited at hearing that an English officer had fired at an alligator. Petitions in great numbers were sent to the Government on the subject, and the people, especially the Brahmans, were with difficulty appeased (*a*). A fair is held at Pushkar in the autumn of every year, when as many as one hundred thousand pilgrims are present, and bathe in the sacred lake.

(*a*) The Rajputana Gazetteer, Vol. II, pp. 67—70.

The Dargah at Ajmere.

This is a tomb in which was buried the pir or saint Khwaja Micaiyin-ud-din Chisti, in the year 1235, shortly before India was invaded by the Emperor Shahâb-ud-din. It is so sacred that pilgrimages are made to it. Akbar himself is said to have performed a pilgrimage on foot to the sacred spot. He erected a large mosque close by. Shah Jehan also built a mosque, the materials of which were of white marble. The edifice is still as fresh as it was on the day it was built, some two hundred and fifty years ago. On the left of this mosque is the tomb of the saint, a square-domed building with two sandal-wood doors, the spoils of Chitore, and a silver arch, the gift of Siwai Jai Singh of Jeypore.

The Arhai-din-kâ-jhompra, or Great Mosque of Ajmere.

This mosque, says General Cunningham, is "one of the earliest and finest monuments of the Mahomedan power in India. Like the great Kutb Masjid at Delhi, the Ajmere mosque was built of the spoils of many Hindu temples, which were thrown down by the bigotry of the conquerors. Its very name, the 'shed of two days and-a-half,' which is the only appellation by which it is now known, would seem to point directly to the astonishing rapidity of its erection, and as this could only have been effected by the free use of the ready dressed materials of prostrated Hindu temples, I accept the popular name as confirmatory proof of the actual origin of the masjid, which is amply attested by an inspection of the edifice itself. The Great Mosque of Ajmere consists of a quadrangle cloistered on all four sides, with a lofty screen wall of seven pointed arches forming a magnificent front to the western side. The side cloisters are mostly ruined; but the whole of the seven noble arches of the screen wall, as well as the grand pillared cloisters behind them, are still standing. Altogether it is the finest and largest specimen of the early Mahomedan mosque that now exists. It is of the same age as the Kutb Mosque at Delhi, but is considerably larger, and in very much better preservation. Externally, it is a square of 259 feet each side, with four peculiar star-shaped towers at the corners. The interior consists of a quadrangle 200 feet by 175, surrounded on all four sides by cloisters of Hindu pillars. The great screen is no less than 11½ feet thick and 56 feet high. I am inclined to believe that the two mosques must have been designed by the same architect, and that even the same masons may have been employed in the decoration of each." "In the Ajmere mosque we have the earliest example of a pair of *muazzin* towers in two small *minars*, which are placed on the top of the screen wall over the great centre arch. This arrangement was impracticable in the

Delhi mosque, as the screen wall is only eight feet thick" (*a*). On one of these minars is an inscription, from which the information is obtained, that the mosque was completed in the reign of the Emperor Altamish, or between A. D. 1211 and 1236. The mosque is a vast pillared hall with five rows of columns, numbered altogether three hundred and forty-four. Each pillar, it is conjectured, is made up of at least two original pillars; no less than seven hundred columns are represented by those now standing, an enormous number, equivalent, in General Cunningham's judgment, to the spoils of from twenty to thirty Hindu temples. It is his opinion that the two great mosques of Delhi and Ajmere belong to a higher and nobler style of art than the Saracenic architects ever reached. "In gorgeous prodigality of ornament, in beautiful richness of tracery, and endless variety of detail, in delicate sharpness of finish, and laborious accuracy of workmanship, all of which are due to the Hindu masons, I think that these two grand Indian mosques may justly vie with the noblest buildings which the world has yet produced. In attributing the design to the Musalman architect, and all the constructive details to the Hindu, I am chiefly influenced by the fact that the arch has never formed part of Hindu structural architecture, although it is found in many specimens of their rock-hewn temples" (*b*).

The Temple and Monastery of Dâdu Panth at Barahana, near the Sambhar Lake.

Dâdu was the founder of a Hindu sect in the sixteenth century. His followers are found in many parts of the country. Dâdu died in the neighbourhood of the lake, and these edifices have been erected to his memory, and to perpetuate his creed. His precepts have been recorded in a book which is held in great veneration by his disciples. These persons eschew idolatry, shave their heads, teach morality, and wander about in all directions preaching the doctrines of Dâdu. The head-quarters of the sect are said to be in the Jeypore State. The armed Nagas are attached to the sect.

The old Royal Palace at Amber, in Jeypore.

For nearly seven centuries Amber was the capital of the Jeypore kingdom, that is, from A.D. 1037 to 1728. The old palace of the great chiefs of this principality is still standing, and commands a grand and picturesque view of the surrounding country. This ancient city, however, is almost abandoned, and its former splendid buildings are falling into ruins.

(*a*) Archæological Survey of India, General Cunningham's Report. Vol. II, pp. 258—261.
(*b*) *Ibid*, p. 263.

The Gutta.

A very sacred shrine dedicated to the sun, on the summit of the hills, about one mile and-a-half to the east of Jeypore. A spring issues from the rocks below the shrine, and falls seventy feet. Its water is regarded as exceedingly sacred, and a tradition prevails among the people fostered by the priest of the temple, that the water is as holy and efficacious as that of the Ganges at Benares or Hurdwar.

The Observatory at Jeypore.

This was erected by Maharajah Siwai Jai Singh II. The instruments are of enormous size, but are in decay, and have probably not been used since the Maharajah's death in 1743.

The Silla Devi Temple.

This temple, reputed to be of great antiquity, is situated within the palace at Amber, the former capital of Jeypore. A goat is daily sacrificed to the goddess, in the place, it is said, of a human victim formerly offered.

The Amberkiswas Shrine.

This is a very old shrine, dedicated to Shiva, and still standing in Amber. It is commonly believed that the city took its name from the sacred shrine.

The Monastery and Shrines of the Dâdu Panthis at Naraina.

The monastery is built of the finest Makrâna marble, and has a very striking appearance. The great enclosure inside is decorated with pillars rising from a platform. In the inner part are deposited various sacred objects, among which are the Dâdu Panth's writings and the bed on which Dâdu lay. The impressions of his feet are also shown.

On the shores of the lake at Naraina is a mosque of considerable beauty, a composite of Mahomedan and Hindu styles. Its five rows of richly carved pillars, differing very greatly in their characteristics, are of Hindu art, having been taken from shrines and temples, and put together by Mahomedan architects according to their own designs. These pillars resemble those at the Kutb near Delhi, and are considered to date from A.D. 961, the era of the temple of the 'Lord of Joy,' in Shekhawatee (*a*).

(*a*) The Rajputana Gazetteer, Vol. II, p. 161.

The Tripolia.

This singular building was erected in A.D. 1603, and is situated at Naraina. It is largely composed of materials taken from older edifices. It has four angles of a ceiling, 'exactly similar to that of the portico of the temple of Baroli, dedicated to Shiva, near the Makundara Pass on the Chambal' (*a*).

Jain Temples at Sangarer.

This ancient spot is seven miles from Jeypore. It contains many old Hindu and Jain buildings, the most remarkable of which is a temple reputed to be more than a thousand years old, constructed of marble and sandstone. Its style resembles that of the celebrated Dilwârà Jain temple on Mount Abu. Foreigners are not admitted into its most sacred parts.

The Charan-padh.

Two miles from Jeypore are, as is supposed, the impressions of the feet of Ram Chandra, over which a shrine was raised in former times, and is, with the Charan-padh, an object of great veneration to Hindus.

The Shrines at Bairât.

Bairât was the ancient capital of Matsya, the name by which the territory of Jeypore was formerly known. It was famous in Hindu writings for being the residence of the five Pându brothers during their twelve years' exile from Indraprastha; and is referred to in the seventh century of our era as being an important city, and having within its circuit several Buddhist monasteries (*b*).

The Jain Temple at Ladorva.

Ladorva was the capital of the Bhâtî rulers before they built Jesalmere. It is now in ruins; but an ancient temple of the Jains is still standing.

The ancient Jain Temples of Jesalmere.

These are situated inside the fort, and are famous for their exquisite sculptures. The oldest dates from the year 1371 (*c*).

The Maha Suttee at Bundee.

This spot is famous for the cremation of the bodies of former chiefs of Bundee, and the burning of many of their wives. Very handsome monuments have been

(*a*) The Rajputana Gazetteer, Vol. II, p. 161.
(*b*) *Ibid*, p. 162.
(*c*) *Ibid*, p. 182.

erected to commemorate these events, on which are recorded not merely the names of the chiefs, but also the number of the unfortunate ladies who at their death performed the terrible rite of suttee. According to these inscriptions, as many as two hundred and thirty-seven women thus voluntarily surrendered their lives on the death of nine chiefs, as follows :—

At the death of	Rao Raja Sattra Sal,	ninety-five	women	were burnt as suttees.
Do.	Rao Raja Bhao Singh,	thirty-five	do.	do.
Do.	Maharaja Jodh Singh,	three	do.	do.
Do.	Rao Raja Ajit Singh,	two	do.	do.
Do.	Rao Bhojh Singh,	two	do.	do.
Do.	Rao Ratan Singh,	one	do.	do.
Do.	Maharaj Bhurt Singh,	twelve	do.	do.
Do.	Rao Kishen Singh,	eighty-four	do.	do.
Do.	Rao Budh Singh,	three	do.	do. (a).

Marriage Customs in Rajputana.

According to Hindu law, no money is allowed to be given by a Hindu on the marriage of a daughter, a law which, among some castes and in some places, is more frequently honoured in the breach than in the observance. The reason of the law is mainfest, and approves itself both to humanity and civilization. It is simply that the Hindu law abhors anything having the appearance of the sale of a girl to her husband. Yet not a few Hindu tribes in their marriage ceremonies are notoriously guilty at the least of such appearance. Rajpoots especially in all parts of the country are accustomed to give large sums of money on the marriage of their daughters, which circumstance has been a fruitful cause of female infanticide, parents preferring to slaughter girls in their infancy to bearing the ruinous burden of procuring costly husbands for them on their attaining a marriageable age. In Rajputana this evil custom of giving a considerable amount of money on the marriage of a young woman is said to prevail among three-fourths of the Rajpoot population, and also among most other Hindu castes. It is important to state, however, that an opposite custom, namely, of giving money on the marriage of young men, is also observed among some tribes. In inferior castes, the bride's mother expects a large present of money from the bridegroom in return for her daughter.

The ceremonies of betrothal and marriage are very curious among Rajputana tribes, and differ greatly in different tribes. The following customs prevail in Jodhpore : Among Rajpoots and Chârans, the bride and bridegroom eat opium

(a) The Rajputana Gazetteer. Vol. I, p. 237.

together in the presence of their caste. With Tailang Brahmans, the bridegroom's father sends a handkerchief to be put on the bride's head. With Sâraswat Brahmans, the bride's father places a ring on the bridegroom's finger. Among all other Brahmans the custom is for the girl's father to make presents of fruit, sugar, cocoanuts, and so forth, to the bridegroom's friends, or to receive them. The Oswâl bankers, at the time of marriage, send a garland of flowers and a ring from the bridegroom's family to the bride. Among other Vaisyas the betrothal is confirmed by simply giving to the other party sugar and cocoanuts. The Jatia Kumhârs bind a thread round the bride's wrist. The general custom among the great majority of the castes as a token of the binding of the contract between the parties, is the exchange of sugar and cocoanuts. At the time of the celebration of the marriage, the bridegroom takes hold of the bride's hand, and together they go round a fire in the centre of the room three times, and then a fourth time, the bride on this occasion walking before the bridegroom. The Srimâli Brahmans wait till the morning after the marriage before encircling the fire, when the bridegroom takes the bride up in his arms, and carries her four times round the fire. The Maheshwari and Panchoti Vaisyas observe a singular custom. The bride's maternal uncle, on the bridegroom entering the house of the bride, catches her up in his arms, and takes her round the bridegroom seven times (*a*).

As every Rajpoot takes a wife from a tribe other than his own, the abduction of the bride, real or professed, is the universal practice. This custom arose in times when a tribe, being dependant for wives on the good-will of neighbouring tribes, found itself thwarted in its matrimonial inclinations through their enmity and hostility, and hence the frequent feuds which arose between them. Although such tribal strifes have largely ceased, yet the manner of forcible abduction continues. "The ceremony may be witnessed in great perfection at any marriage in high life, when the bridegroom arrives with his wedding band of armed kinsmen, who clash their arms and rush in with a shout upon the bride's party" (*b*).

(*a*) The Rajputana Gazetteer, Vol. II, p. 251.
(*b*) *Ibid*, Vol. I, p 69.

CHAPTER II.

THE BRAHMANICAL TRIBES.

SEC. I.—BRAHMANS OF PUSHKAR. SEC. II.—BRAHMANS OF BIKANEER. SEC III—BRAHMANS OF KARAULI. SEC. IV.—BRAHMANS OF MARWAR. SEC. V.—BRAHMANS OF MALLANI. SEC VI.—BRAHMANS OF SANCHORE. SEC. VII.—BRAHMANS OF JESALMERE. SEC. VIII.—BRAHMANS OF THE RAJPUTANA DESERT. SEC. IX.—BRAHMANS OF JEYPORE. SEC. X.—BRHAMANS OF AJMERE-MERWARA. SEC. XI.—BRAHMANS OF BANSWARA. SEC. XII.—BRAHMANS OF BHURTPORE. SEC. XIII.—BRAHMANS OF BUNDEE. SEC. XIV.—BRAHMANS OF DHOLPORE.

The Brahmans of Ajmere hold no social intercourse with those of Merwara, the chief reason being, perhaps, that the latter eat animal food. They hold lands in nearly all the villages in these States with the important privilege of paying no revenue for the same. They seldom cultivate the soil themselves (*a*).

The hills in the vicinity of Kalinjar, Laroth, and Bhadan were, according to tradition, first occupied by Brahmanical tribes.

Section I.—Brahmans of Pushkar.

The Brahmans of Pushkar are divided into two branches, the Barâ Bâs and the Chhotâ Bâs, between whom a great feud has always existed. The former are regarded as having preceded the latter in the town; but they have both been there for many generations. A charter of the Emperor Jehangir is extant, referring to the division of offerings by these two tribes, and endeavouring to heal the animosity between them by ordering two-thirds to be given to the older tribe, and one-third to the younger, which rule still exists.

The entire population of Pushkar numbers nearly four thousand persons, of whom the greater part are Brahmans of the two sects just referred to. There seems good reason to believe that the Barâ Bâs are older than the Chhotâ Bâs (*b*).

(*a*) Gazetteer of Ajmere-Merwara, by Mr. J. D. LaTouche, p. 32.

(*b*) The Rajputana Gazetteer. Vol. II, p. 70.

1. *The Barâ Bâs Brahmans of Pushkar.*

The tradition of these Brahmans is, that they are descended from Parâsar, father of Veda Vyâsa, through Bhopat, who, in common belief, was a Mair. The *sewaks*, or priests of the Jain temples, intermarry with the Barâ Bâs Brahmans, which is a very remarkable circumstance, seeing that the Jains are not Brahmans, but Vaisyas. It is needless to add, therefore, that other Brahmans decline to hold intercourse with the Pushkar sect.

2. *The Chhotâ Bâs Brahmans of Pushkar.*

These Brahmans are divided into the following four clans :—

1. Gaur.	3. Gujrâti.
2. Sanâdh.	4. Raj Purohit.

The Chhotâ Bâs Brahmans are *purohits*, or family priests, to the Rajas of Jeypore, Bikaneer, Bhurtpore, and Dholpore (*a*). They have no writing or tradition stating when they first came to Pushkar.

Section II.—Brahmans of Bikaneer.

The Brahmans of Bikaneer are chiefly of two classes, namely :—

1. Pokarna. These are ten times more numerous than any other Brahmanical tribe in the State. They are traders and agriculturists, and are an energetic, hard-working people. Astrologers are of this clan.

2. Paliwâl. Enterprising trading agriculturists, inhabiting twelve villages west of Bikaneer. Many of this tribe emigrated into British territory a few years ago.

The priests of the Darbar, or Court, as of Râthor Rajpoots generally, are Kanoujiya Brahmans of the Sanâdhiya branch. The teachers of the Shâstras are Gour Brahmans.

Section III.—Brahmans of Karauli.

The Brahmanical tribes of Karauli are the most numerous of all the tribes in the State. They are mostly small traders, and convey their goods from place to place on pack-cattle. They bear various designations, such as :—

1. Borârs or Ladeniâs (carriers of merchandize). In addition to trading they are often "the village money-lenders, or cultivators, especially of hemp, which they prepare in large quantities, and work up into *tât*, the coarse cloth of which their packing bags are made. They carry salt from Lâmbar, sugar from

(*a*) Gazetteer of Ajmere-Merwara, by Mr. J. D. LaTouche, p 58.

Agra, cotton, ghi (clarified butter), and piece-goods, to the marts, where they are wanted" (*a*). The Borârs are mostly Kanoujiya Brahmans of the Sanâdhiya sub-tribe. They are nearly all able to read and write.

2. Brinjârâs. Although bearing this name, these Brahmans are very unlike the wandering Brinjârâ tribes of the Dekhan.

3. Haiwâsis. These have been carriers of merchandize for many generations, and some of them journey over a wide extent of country. Not a few feed their cattle on the waste lands of Shopur, Badowra, Duma in Gondwana, and other parts of Central India, while still keeping up intercourse with their brethren in Karauli. The Haiwâsis of this State are settled at Laknipur, in Mâchilpur. There are members of the tribe in Bâri, Ulwar, Gwalior, and on the banks of the Nerbuddha. The Haiwâsis mostly worship Raghunâth. Some of the tribe in Marwar have become converts to Mahomedanism.

4. Gujrâti Brahmans. Of these, there are about sixty families in Karauli. They are worshippers of Vishnu.

5. Gor or Gaur Brahmans. A few families.

6. Gor Beas. A few families.

7. Nandwâni. These are Brahmans from Marwar, and are found in the city of Karauli and in all the large villages. They are active traders. They have a higher social position than the Borars (*b*).

Section IV.—Brahmans of Marwar.

These are said, by Major Walter, to be subdivided as follows:—

1. Tailang.
2. Parik.
3. Sankhwâl.
4. Gor or Gaur.
5. Kanoujya.
6. Pushkarna.
7. Sâwug.
8. Srimâli.
9. Sâraswat.
10. Khandelwâl.
11. Sarwaria.
12. Gujrâti.
13. Parohit.
14. Daima.
15. Gujar-gor.
16. Sanâwar.
17. Nadwâni.
18. Lachora.
19. Palliwâl (*c*).
20. Asopa.

This is, however, a very confused and unsatisfactory list of subdivisions. The Parohits are simply village priests, and may belong to any of the Brahmanical tribes. The Sarwarias form one of the great branches of the Kanoujya Brahmans; as also do the Sanâwars or Sanâdhs.

(*a*) Gazetteer of the Karauli State, by Capt. P. W. Powlett, p. 17.
(*b*) *Ibid*, p. 18.
(*c*) Gazetteer of Marwar, by Major C. K. M. Walter, Political Agent, Marwar, p. 24.

Asopa Brahmans have held important posts in the Marwar Darbar. Pushkarna Brahmans held the offices of Dewan and Bukhshi in the reign of Moharaja Takht Singh. Among the Tailang Brahmans the custom prevails of the father sending a handkerchief for the decoration of the head of the girl who is about to espouse his son. A Sâraswat Brahman father places a ring on the finger of the youth who is about to be his son-in-law. A Srimâli Brahman bridegroom carries his bride four times round a fire lit in the centre of the room, on the morning after the first marriage ceremony. The Srimâlis are not cultivators in Mallâni, but traders on a small scale.

Section V.—Brahmans of Mallâni.

In Mállâni, Joshis, or astrologers, are very numerous. Instead of following the uncertain pursuit of astrology, however, they are, for the most part, engaged in trade and agriculture. They enjoy special privileges, paying neither export nor import dues, and only a fourth part of their produce as revenue. The Paliwâl Brahmans came originally to Mallâni with the Râthors. The Sârsat or Sâraswat Brahmans have only recently entered the State from Bikaneer. They are the priests of the Jâts, and are cultivators and beggars. The Râjgur Brahmans are family priests of the Thakurs of Mallâni. One of their duties is, on the death of the head of a family, to take his ashes to the Ganges and to throw them into the stream. Their lands are rent-free.

The Lohânas are trading Brahmans in Mallâni, paying less duty on goods than other castes. They are low in social rank, and eat meat and drink spirits. They are not treated with such consideration as the Joshis.

The Bhojaks are beggars, and cooks in the families of Oswâls. They are worshippers of Shiva, but are lax in principle, and readily pay their devotions in the Jain temples. The Bhojaks are inferior Brahmans.

The Kârtakias are low Brahmans who receive the clothes thrown over dead persons when burnt; and eat the food given in charity during twelve days after the death of any one (*a*).

The Srimâli Brahmans are strict in the observance of their caste rules. They will not work in the fields, but engage in trade in a small way, and of course, like most Brahmans, rigidly adhering to caste, are incorrigible beggars.

Section VI.—Brahmans of Sanchore.

This district is almost exclusively populated by Brahmans, who bear the designation of Sanchora Brahmans.

(*a*) Gazetteer of Mallâni, by Major C. K. M. Walter, p. 66.

Section VII.—Brahmans of Jesalmere.

These belong to two classes, the Paliwâls and Pokarnas or Pushkarnas. who are the principal sects of Brahmans in the State of Bikaneer. In numbers the Paliwâls equal the Rajpoot tribes, while they far surpass them in wealth. Tod considers that they are the descendants of the ancient Pali or pastoral tribes of this region. They never marry out of their tribe. They worship the bridle of a horse (*a*).

The Pokarnas are numerous in Marwar, Bikaneer, and Jesalmere. As to their origin, there is a tradition that they were formerly Beldars, and as such excavated the Lake Pushkar or Pokar, for which service they were raised into the rank of Brahmans, and permitted to bear the designation of Pokarnas. They worship the khodala, or pickaxe (*b*).

In this State, besides the above Brahmans, there are others of the following tribes, namely:—Srimâli, Joshi, Râjgur or Kesuria, and Gujar-gor.

Section VIII.—Brahmans of the Rajputana Desert.

The most numerous Brahmans of this region are Vaishnavis, who are agriculturists, cowherds, and to some extent traders. They are found in greatest numbers in Dhât. Their dead are buried near the thresholds of their houses. The tribe is also settled in Marwar, Mallâni, and elsewhere.

Section IX.—Brahmans of Jeypore.

In comparison with other States in Rajputana, Brahmans are most numerous in Jeypore, and are engaged in both secular and religious pursuits. From the greater number of Brahmans residing in Jeypore, we are not to conclude, says Tod, "that her princes were more religious than their neighbours, but, on the contrary, that they were greater sinners" (*c*). Most of the Brahmans of this State are Bâgras, an inferior order, many of whom are agriculturists. Brahmans of a higher rank officiate at temples, or are employed in the public service.

Section X.—Brahmans of Ajmere-Merwara.

These number nearly twenty thousand persons in this province, and enjoy special privileges in the villages, in which they hold lands free from revenue, which they are too proud to cultivate. They are an exclusive race, and as they eat meat, keep themselves apart from other Brahmans.

(*a*) Tod's Rajasthan, Vol. II, p. 262.
(*b*) *Ibid.*
(*c*) *Ibid*, p. 397.

Section XI.—Brahmans of Banswara.

In this small State the Brahmans are well represented, and belong, it is said, to as many as twenty-two separate tribes. The capital has a total population of a little more than six thousand persons, of whom one-fifth are Brahmans.

Section XII.—Brahmans of Bhurtpore.

The Brahmans number about seven per cent. of the entire population of Bhurtpore. Many of them are officials of the Native Government, and in the houses of merchants, bankers, chiefs, and others. The following Brahmanical tribes have their representatives in the State :—

Brahmanical Tribes of Bhurtpore.

1. Gour. These are numerous.
2. Kanyakubja. A few only.
3. Utkal Brahmans from Orissa. A few.
4. Sâraswati. In considerable numbers.
5. Maithala. A few.
6. Nagar Brahmans from Gujerat. A few.
7. Maharashtra. A few.
8. Kashmiri. A few (*a*).

Section XIII.—Brahmans of Bundee.

These are engaged in various occupations, as Government officials, as cultivators, and as headmen of villages ; while all are more or less educated. The chief minister of the State is a Nâgar Brahman. The following tribes are represented in Bundee :—

Brahmanical Tribes of Bundee.

1. Sadu.
2. Gour.
3. Sanadhiya.
4. Parikh.
5. Gujar.
6. Daima.
7. Paliwâl.
8. Nâgar.
9. Sâraswati.
10. Sikhwal.

Section XIV.—Brahmans of Dholpore.

In this small State there are thirty-six thousand Brahmans, of whom as many as twenty-seven thousand cultivate upwards of forty-three thousand acres of land. The Golapurah Brahmans occupy twenty-two villages. They profess to be Pâtakh Brahmans, and state that their ancestors entered this district in the middle of the thirteenth century, having come from Palli in Bhurtpore. The Sanadhiya branch of the Kanyakubja Brahmans are the headmen of fifty-one villages.

(*a*) The Rajputana Gazetteer, Vol. I, p. 160.

CHAPTER III.

THE RAJPOOT TRIBES.

I.—CHAUHAN. II.—HARA. III.—RATHOR. IV.—JODHA. V.—JOHIYA. VI.—SILKAWAT. VII.—BIRAMOT. VIII.—BIJAWAT. IX.—SISAWAT. X.—KITAWAT. XI.—TENDO. XII.—MOHIL. XIII.—NARBHANA. XIV.—BHADAURIA. XV.—BHAURECHA. XVI.—DHANAIREA. XVII.—BAGRECHA. XVIII.—KOMBAWAT. XIX.—LUNAWAT. XX.—RANAWAT. XXI.—DULAWAT. XXII.—JHALA. XXIII.—BARGUJAR. XXIV.—SISODIYA. XXV.—GAHLOT. XXVI.—SANKLA. XXVII.—ASAYACH. XXVIII.—CHANDRAWAT. XXIX.—SENGAR.

Râjisthân, or Rajputana, is the country *par excellence* of the Rajpoot tribes, in which, for many ages, they have held extensive dominion. In a former work I have written at length on many of these tribes, and therefore shall consider it incumbent on me now, only to furnish such additional information about those inhabiting Rajputana as I have been able to gather (*a*).

It seems to be generally admitted, that the chiefs of Rajputana, "as a class, are superior to the present fruits of our own institutions in India. They are more inclined to mix with Europeans, and enjoy their society and sports, and are freer from prejudice than any other people in India" (*b*). The Rajpoots are fond of excitement, a disposition produced, perhaps, by the feudal system under which they live. Nevertheless, with all their restlessness and turbulence, in the opinion of Colonel Tod, they possess 'in an eminent degree both loyalty and patriotism.'

The Rajpoot tribes in all the States of Rajputana are divisible into three classes: 1, landholders; 2, cultivators, or tillers of the ground; 3, servants, agents, and the like. The landholders include the old hereditary aristocracy.

Among the Rajpoots of Marwar, at the ceremony of betrothal, the young bridegroom and bride partake of opium together. The same pernicious custom also prevails with the Châran tribe.

(*a*) "Hindu Tribes and Castes," by the author—the Kshatriya or Rajpoot Tribes. Vol. I, Part II, Chapters I—XIII, pp 115—243.

(*b*) History of Mewar, by Captain J. C. Brookes, p. 104.

The social position of these tribes in Rajputana, at the present day, is depicted in these words of Colonel Tod: "The poorest Rajpoot of this day," he says, "retains all the pride of ancestry, often his sole inheritance. He scorns to hold the plough, or to use his lance but on horseback. In these aristocratic ideas he is supported by his reception among his superiors, and the respect paid to him by his inferiors. The honours and privileges, and the gradations of rank, among the vassals of the Rána's house, exhibit a highly artificial and refined state of society. Each of the superior rank is entitled to a banner, kettle-drums preceded by heralds and silver maces, with peculiar gifts and personal honours, in commemoration of some exploit of their ancestors" (*a*).

I. *Chauhân.*

The fort and city of Ajmere were founded, says the local tradition, in the year 145 A. D., by Raja Aja, commonly known as Ajapâl, descended from Anala, the first of the Chauhân race. The Chauhân kings reigned in Ajmere until the end of the twelfth century. In 1193, Mahomed Ghori took possession of the city; but it was not finally annexed to the Mahomedan empire of Delhi until 1195, when the country was once more invaded, and Kutb-ud-dîn Aibeg, viceroy of Mahomed Ghori, fought with the usurper Hemrâj, and having killed him and defeated his army, destroyed completely the remaining power of the ancient dynasty (*b*).

It is very remarkable that although the Chauhâns governed Ajmere for upwards of a thousand years, yet that so few of the tribe are now to be found there. "They must be looked for," says Mr J. D. Latouche, Compiler of the Gazetteer of Ajmere-Merwara, "in Hârâvati, in Ulwar, and in the desert of Nagar Parkhar, whither they have been pushed by the Râthors, who have occupied their place as the ruling tribe, and who in numbers, wealth, and power greatly preponderate over the other Rajpoot clans who hold land in the district" (*c*).

The Chauhâns have colonies in Marwar, Bhurtpore, Jesalmere, and Mallâni. They have distinguished families in Looe Bah and Sanchore. The Chauhâns of Baidla and Kotario, in the Oodaipore valley, are, says Tod, chiefs of the first rank. The chief of Parsoli is also a Chauhân.

The Gogawat clan is descended from the famous Goga, who defended the Sutlej in the earliest recorded Mahomedan invasion. 'Both Goga and his steed

(*a*) Tod's Rajasthan—Madras Edition—Vol. I, p. 123.
(*b*) General Cunningham's Archæological Survey of India. Vol. II, p. 258.
(*c*) Gazetteer of Ajmere-Merwara, by Mr. J. D. Latouche, p. 28.

Jawadia are immortal in Rajasthan.' The Gogawats are among the most ancient tribes of the desert.

The Narbhans are another clan of this tribe. They formerly had possession of Oodaipore, which they held for a long period.

In Banswara are eleven Chauhân clans, three of which are as follows :—

1. Madawat.—These are of Metwala, and are a junior branch of the Molân family.

2. Hathyot.—This clan belongs to Arthuna, and has also sprung from the Molâns.

3. Keringot.—A clan which came originally from Bankora in Dungarpore. They have possession of the Ganora estate.

The tribe is numerous in Bundee. In Dungarpore eight of the principal landholders are of this tribe.

The Chauhâns succeeded the Tuars in Malwee, and reigned there one hundred and sixty-seven years.

II. Hâra.

The Hâras inhabit the country, called after them, Hârâvati, embracing the two States of Boondi and Kotah, and intersected by the Chumbul. Their founder. according to Tod, was Ishtpâl, descended from Manik Rae, the Chauhân king of Ajmere, who, A. D. 685, "sustained the first shock of the Islamite arms." Ishtpâl was severely wounded in battle while resisting the invading army of Mahmud of Ghizni. "His limbs, which lay dissevered, as the story goes, were collected by Sûrabai ; and the goddess sprinkling them with the 'water of life,' he arose. Hence the name Hâra, which his descendants bore, from *har*, or 'bones' thus collected ; but more likely from having lost (*hara*) Asi" (*a*). Boondî, the capital of the Hâras, was built by Rae Dewa, about the year 1342, by whom the country received the designation of Hârâvati.

The tribe has the following clans :—

The Hâra Clans.

1. The Kombawat Clan—descended from the famous Aloo Hâra, son of Har-raj. Aloo Hâra had twenty-four castles on the Pathar.
2. The Bhojawat Clan—also descended from Aloo Hâra.
3. The Harpalpota Clan—descended from Harpal. son of Samarsi.

(*a*) Tod's Rajasthan—Madras Edition—Vol. II. p. 420

4. The Norangpota Clan—descended from Norang, son of the renowned Napûji.
5. The Tharad Clan—descended from Tharad, another son of Napûji.
6. The Meoh Clan—descended from Meoji, great grandson of Hamoo, ruler of Boondî in the fifteenth century.
7. The Sawant Clan—descended from Sawant, brother of Meoji.
8. The Novarmapota Clan—descended from Novarma, grandson of Hamoo.
9. The Jailawat Clan—descended from Jaita, grandson of Hamoo.
10. The Nimawat Clan—descended from Nima, grandson of Hamoo.
11. The Akawat Clan—descended from Ako, great grandson of Hamoo.
12. The Udâwat Clan—descended from Udoh, great grandson of Hamoo.
13. The Chandawat Clan—descended from Chanda, great grandson of Hamoo.
14. The Râma Clan—descended from Râm Singh, son of Arjûn.
15. The Akhirajpota Clan—descended from Akhiraj, son of Arjûn.
16. The Jessa Clan—descended from Kandîl, son of Arjûn.
17. The Indarsalot Clan—descended from Indar Singh, who founded Indargurh.
18. The Berisalot Clan—descended from Beri Sal, who founded Bahran and Filodi.
19. The Mokhimsingot Clan—descended from Mokhim Singh, who had Anterdeh.

The Hâras of Kotah, descended from Madhu Singh, the founder of the Kotah State, have the patronymic of Madhani, and are thus distinguished from all other Hâra clans.

III. Râthor.

On the destruction of Kanauj, the capital of the ancient kingdom of the same name, the Râthors abandoned their country, which they had governed with wonderful energy so long, and entering the barren wastes of Marwar, founded a new kingdom there. "The Râthors of Ajmere have the same customs and characteristics as their brethren in Marwar. They are still warlike and indolent, and great consumers of opium. Each man carriés at least a dagger, and, except under extreme pressure, none will touch a plough" (*a*). The village of Khori held by the Râthors was once in the possession of the Mers, but was taken from them by these Rajpoots. This tribe has eighty-three Bhumia holdings in

(*a*) Gazetteer of Ajmere-Merwara, by Mr. J. D. Latouche, p. 29.

Ajmere. All the talukdars or great landholders of the district, with few exceptions, are Râthors, descended from Seoji.

The Râthors of Bikaneer have sprung from the Râthors of Marwar, and were established there by Bikâ, the son of Jodhain, in 1459. The Maharaja of Bikaneer claims to be the head of the tribe in that territory. The Râthors of that principality are divided into the following clans :—

The Râthor Clans of Bikaneer.

1. The Bikâ Clan—descended from Bîkâ, the founder of the Bikaneer State. with nine principal families :—1, Rajwi ; 2, Ratan Singot ; 3, Sringot ; 4, Kishan Singot ; 5, Umrawat ; 6, Nârnot ; 7, Bhîmrajot ; 8, Gharsiot ; 9, Pirthi Râjot. The chief seats of the clan are at Mahajin, Jessanoh, Baie, and Hyadesir.

2. The Bidâwat Clan—descended from Bidâ, Bikâ's brother, with six principal families :—1, Manohardasat ; 2, Tejsiot ; 3, Khagârot ; 4, Pirthi Râjot ; 5, Keshodâsot ; 6, Mân Singot. Their country extends along part of the Marwar and Shekhawati frontiers. They are especially addicted to plundering. Their chief seats are at Bedasir and Saondwa.

3. The Karmsîot Clan—descended from Karmsi, a less distinguished brother of Bikâ, a small clan. Their chief seat is at Nokho.

4. The Kândhalot Clan—descended from Kândhal, Bikâ's uncle and chief supporter, consisting of three great families :—1, Raolot ; 2, Barînrot ; 3, Saindasot.

5. The Mandhlâwat Clan—descended from Mandhal, a less distinguished uncle of Bikâ. They have ten villages. Their chief seat is at Saroonda.

6. The Rupâwat Clan—descended from Rûpji, another uncle of Bikâ (*a*). They possess ten villages. Their chief seat is at Badilah.

7. The Randhirot Clan—possessing one village.

8. The Mândlot Clan—occupying three villages.

9. The Ranmalot Clan—holding one village.

10. The Jaitmalot Clan—possessing one village.

11. The Kundalia Clan—with two villages.

12. The Udâwat Clan—holding four villages.

13. The Nâthal Clan—occupying two villages.

14. The Patâwat Clan—with one village.

15. The Gohel Clan—with one village.

16. The Benirot Clan.

(*a*) Gazetteer of Bikaneer, by Captain P. W. Powlett, p 111.

The ruling chief of Marwar is at the head of the Râthor tribe in that State. There is good ground for the belief that, prior to the conquest of Marwar by the Râthors, that country had been governed at various periods by Jâts, Bheels, and Meenas. The Râthors abandoned Kanauj after the destruction of their capital by Shahab-ud-din in 1194. Some of them migrated westerly, and gradually conquered the small chieftains who formerly ruled over Marwar. The Râthors finally gained possession of Marwar under Rao Chanda, in the year 1382. His grandson, Jodha, founded the present city of Jodhpore, and made it the capital of the Marwar or Jodhpore State.

The Thakurs or great landholders of Ganora and Bednore, in Mewar, belong to the Mairtia clan of Râthors.

Mallâni claims to be the cradle of the Râthors in the west; for, on the downfall of Kanauj, Asthân, the great grandson of the last monarch, abandoning his native country, wandered with his followers to the west, and at the end of the twelfth century, captured from the Gohel Rajpoots the town of Kher, near the Luni, and took possession of the district of Mewo, now called Mallâni. The Gohels had seized the territory from the Bheels twenty years before. On being thus dispossessed the Gohels moved on to Bhaunagar, on the gulf of the Mâhi, where they are still a numerous body. The Râthors increased their principality in the time of Mallinath by the addition of Gûra and Nagar, which they conquered from the Soras. The Barmer District of Mallâni, at the date of the foundation of the Râthor rule under Asthân, was in the hands of the Sanklas, from whom it was taken by the Chauhâns, who, on their turn, were overcome by the Râthors, who annexed the district permanently (*a*).

The Râthors are very powerful in Marwar, where they are divided into the following clans:—

The Râthor Clans of Marwar.

1. The Jodha Clan—holding the chieftainships of Khari-ka-dewa, Chanpur, and Bûdsû.

2. The Champawat Clan—holding the chieftainships of Ahwa, Pokurn, Kâtoh, Palri, Hursola, Degode, Rohit, Jawula, Suttana, and Tingari.

3. The Kûmpawat Clan—holding the chieftainships of Asope, Kuntaleo, Chundawal, Siriari, Kharlo, Hursore, Bulloo, Bajoria, Sûrpura, Dewureo, Buggori, Gujsingpûra, and Roat.

4. The Mandlot Clan—holding the chieftainship of Sârunda.

(*a*) The Rajputana Gazetteer, Vol. II, p. 265.

5. The Pattawat Clan—holding the chieftainships of Kurnichari, Baroh. and Desnokh.
6. The Lakhawat Clan.
7. The Balawat Clan—holding the chieftainship of Dhûnara.
8. The Jaitmalot Clan—holding the chieftainship of Palasni.
9. The Karnot Clan—holding the chieftainship of Lûnawas.
10. The Rûpawat Clan—holding the chieftainship of Chûtela.
11. The Dûngerot Clan.
12. The Sandawat Clan.
13. The Mandnot Clan.
14. The Birot Clan.
15. The Jagmalot Clan.
16. The Hampawat Clan.
17. The Saktawat Clan.
18. The Urivalot Clan.
19. The Ketseot Clan.
20. The Satrosalot Clan.
21. The Tejmalot Clan (*a*)

A branch of the Râthors is settled in Jesalmere, and also in Jhalawar. There are a few also in Bhurtpore.

Talwara and Aorwara, in Banswara, are held by two branches of the Mairtia Râthors. The Talwara Pass is in their hands, and they are responsible for its security.

The chief of Kusalgarh is of this tribe, and is said to be descended from Jodh Singh, the founder of Jodhpore. The appellation of Ranawat is applied to the members of the ruling family of the State. This district has eight principal landholders, all of whom are Râthor Rajpoots. The tribe is also strong in Bundee. It has some representatives in Dungarpore, and one of the principal landowners is connected with it.

IV. Jodha.

The Jodha tribe, descended from Jodha, the founder of the Jodhpore State; is subdivided into a number of clans, as follows :—

The Jodha Clans.

1. The Santal or Satil Clan—having the chieftainship of Satulmere.

(*a*) Tod's Rajasthan—Madras Edition—Vol. II, p. 15.

2. The Mairtia Clan—having the chieftainships of Reah, Gahorah, Mehtri, and Mairta. The Mairtias are descended from Dûdoh, a son of Jodha. The Jaimalot and Jagmalot Clans, says Tod, are descended from Jaimal and Jagmal, two sons of Bîram, a son of Dûdoh.

3. The Bharmalot Clan—having the chieftainship of Bai Bhilara.

4. The Seorajot Clan—having the chieftainship of Dhûnara, on the Lûni.

5. The Karmsot Clan—having the chieftainship of Keonsir.

6. The Raimalot Clan.

7. The Samatseot Clan—having the chieftainship of Dewaroh.

8. The Bîdawat Clan—having the chieftainship of Bîdavati, in the Nagore District (*a*).

Jodha, the first ruler of Marwar, was succeeded by his son, Sûrjoh, or Sûraj Mal, who, through his sons, originated the following clans :—

The Sûrjoh or Sûraj Mal Clans.

1. The Udawat Clan—having chieftainships at Neemaj, Jytarun, Goondochi, Chundawal, Kooahaman, Chundawal, Khada, Marot, Biratea, and Raepore. It has also settlements in Mewar.

2. The Sagawat Clan—with settlements at Burwoh.

3. The Priagot Clan.

4. The Narawat Jodha Clan—a branch is established at Pachpahar, in Haronti (*b*).

V. *Johiya.*

These are a very ancient tribe, formerly known as Yaudheyas, "who probably contended with Alexander, before whose time they were, it is believed, established on the banks of the Sutlej. Yaudheya coins, as old as the first century of the Christian era, have been found near that river (Cunningham's Ancient Geography, Vol. I, p. 245). The Johiyas are by no means extinct, as Tod imagined. Many of them are Musalmans ; but some in the Sirsa District are still Hindus. According to General Cunningham, they formerly held much of the country west and south-west of Bhatner ; and their chief places were Kharbara, Sahankot, and Badopul, which the Râhtors took from them. There are three sections of the tribe : 1, the Admera ; 2, the Lakvira,—who are settled on the banks of the Sutlej ; and 3, the Madhera, who, together with the representative of the house of Madhu, the founder of the clan, are, for the most part,

(*a*) Tod's Rajasthan—Madras Edition—Vol. II, p 18.

(*b*) *Ibid*, p. 20.

subjects of the Bikaneer State. The boundary of these two divisions is still the bank of the old Sutlej" (a).

VI. *Silkawat.*

A numerous class of *bhûmias* or landholders in Mehwo and Rardurro, in Marwar, descendants of Siluk or Silks.

VII. *Biramot.*

A numerous tribe at Saitroo, Sewandh, and Daichoo, in Marwar, descended from Birumdeo, the son of Siluk.

VIII. *Bijawat.*

Numerous at Saitroo, Sewandh, and Daichoo, in Marwar, descended from Birumdeo, the son of Siluk.

IX. *Sisawat.*

A tribe in Marwar.

X. *Kitawat.*

A tribe in Marwar.

XI. *Tendo.*

An ancient tribe in Marwar.

XII. *Mohil.*

A Chauhân tribe, descended from Manik Rae of Ajmere. The Râthors took Nagore from them in the fifteenth century.

XIII. *Narbhana.*

A Chauhân tribe, descended from Manik Rae of Ajmere.

XIV. *Bhadauria.*

A Chauhân tribe, descended from Manik Rae of Ajmere. Their appanage on the Chumbul still bears their name. In the early part of the last century the Bhadaurias under Rajah Kalyan Singh took possession of Dholpore, which they held till 1761, after the battle of Paniput, when they lost it.

XV. *Bhaurecha.*

A Chauhân tribe, descended from Manik Rae of Ajmere.

(a) Gazetteer of the Bikaneer State, by Captain P. W. Powlett, p. 123.

XVI. *Dhanairea.*

A Chauhân tribe, descended from Manik Rae of Ajmere. They formerly held Shahabad.

XVII. *Bâgrecha.*

A Chauhân tribe, descended from Manik Rae of Ajmere.

XVIII. *Kombawat.*

A tribe of allodial *bhûmias* or landholders in Mewar.

XIX. *Lûnawat.*

A tribe of allodial *bhûmias* or landholders in Mewar. They are proprietors of lands bordering on Oguna, Panora, and other tracts in the Aravulli. The Lûnawats are like the Dûlawats, descended from Lakha Rana, chief of Chitore in A. D. 1373.

XX. *Ranawat.*

A tribe of allodial *bhûmias* or landholders in Mewar. The ancestor of the Raja of Shapoora, a descendant of Rana Udya Singh, was of this tribe.

XXI. *Dûlawat.*

A tribe of allodial *bhûmias* or landholders, in the high lands bordering on Oguna, Panora, and other tracts in the Aravulli. The Dûlawats are descended from Lakha Rana, chief of Chitore, in A. D. 1373.

XXII. *Jhala.*

The chiefs of Sadri, Dailwarra, and Gogoonda, in Mewar, are of this tribe. It is also found in Jesalmere. The ruling family of Jhalâwâr is of the Jhala tribe. These Rajpoots came originally from Kattywar, of which they were once the rulers.

XXIII. *Bargûjar.*

An important tribe in Jeypore and Marwar. The Bargûjars are proprietors of twenty-five villages in the State of Dholpore.

XXIV. *Sisodiya.*

This is properly a branch of the Gahlot or Grahilot tribe. The Rana of Oodaipore or Mewar is a Sisodiya. The Emperor Shah Jehan presented the *pargannah* or barony of Phulia, which was formerly part of Ajmere, to the Raja of Shahpoora, a member of the royal family of Oodaipore.

The tribe also has possession of the *pargannah* of Sâwar, to the south-east of the district, the gift of Jehangir to its ancestor Gokul Dass, who had the reputation of having been wounded eighty-four times in the wars of that emperor.

The Râwals or native chiefs of Banswara have sprung from the Sisodiyas of Dungarpore, from whom they separated in the year 1530. Previously to that period Bagâr or the two States of Dungarpore and Banswara belonged to this tribe. Formerly, in the Banswara State, eight first class nobles of the Sisodiya and Chauhân tribes sat on the right of the throne, and eight Râthors of the same rank sat on the left, of whom only three families are remaining. The Sisodiyas in this State are divided into eight branches. There are a few members of the tribe in Bundee.

The Sisodiyas of Dungarpore, of whom the Maha Rawal is the head, claim to be descended from the elder branch of the Oodaipore family. We learn from Tod that these entered the State as emigrants from Meywar at the end of the twelfth century. Sir John Malcolm states that they came from Meywar about three hundred years ago.

There are also some members of this tribe in possession of lands at Nepoli, in Ajmere (*a*). They occupy four villages in Bikaneer. The tribe has families in Mallâni. Several of the principal chiefs of Oodaipore besides the Maharana, are attached to this tribe. There is also a branch of the tribe at Jaharawar. The principal clans of Sisodiyas in Meywar are as follows:—

Clans of Sisodiyas in Meywar.

1. Chandâwat. In former times the Chandâwats and Sakhtâwats were rival tribes in Meywar, of great power and importance. Their feuds, says Tod, have been the destruction of Meywar. The chief of Saloombra is the present head of the tribe. A few Chandâwats occupy a village in Bikaneer. Two of the chief landholders of Dungarpore are of this tribe.

2. Sakhtâwat. These are fewer in number than the Chandâwats; but they have the 'reputation of greater bravery and more genius.' The chiefs of Bheendir and Bansi are of this clan.

3. Sangâwat. The chief of Deogarh is of the Sangâwat clan.

4. Megâwat. The Rawat of Beygoo is of this clan.

5. Jagâwat. The Rawat of Amait is a Jagâwat.

6. Sarangdeote. The Rawat of Kanorh is of the Sarangdeote clan.

7. Kishenâwat. The Rawats of Bhynsror and Korabur are of this clan.

(*a*) Gazetteer of Ajmere-Merwara, by Mr. J. D. Latouche, p. 29.

XXV. The Gahlot Tribe.

This tribe is descended from a child born in a cave, whose mother, a Ranee of the royal house of Balabhi, was the only person who escaped when that city was sacked. The word *gahlot* means 'cave-born.' The Gahlots are one of the thirty-six royal Rajpoot tribes (*a*).

There is a small community of Gahlots in Bikaneer, Marwar, Mallâni, and Jesalmere.

XXVI. Sânklâ.

The mother of Bîkâ, the founder of the Bikaneer State, was a member of this tribe. He was the sixth son of Jodha, Rao of Marwar, who originated the State of Jodhpore. The Sânklâs are a branch of the Pramara tribe. They were expelled from Kher in Mallâni by the Chauhâns, who in their turn were subdued by the Râthors. Chiefs of Poogul, and in Marwar, are of this tribe.

XXVII. Asayach.

This tribe possesses one village in Bikaneer.

XXVIII. Chandrâwat.

The Chandrâwats are landholders in Jeypore. A small number occupy a village in Bikaneer. There is a branch in Jhalawar.

XXIX. Sengar.

A few Sengar Rajpoots have established themselves in the village of Kallianpura in Karauli. The chiefs occupy a small mud fort. The Sengars are established at Jagmohanpur, on the Jumna.

(*a*) *See* a detailed Account of this Tribe in the Author's "Hindu Tribes and Castes," Vol. I, pp. 125—135.

CHAPTER IV.

THE RAJPOOT TRIBES—(*Continued*).

XXX.—YADU, JADU, OR JADON. XXXI.—BHATI. XXXII—SODA. XXXIII.—KACHWAHA. XXXIV.—SHEKHAWAT. XXXV.—DEWAL. XXXVI.—SALANKHI. XXXVII.—BHAGELA. XXXVIII.—INDAR. XXXIX.—BIRPURA. XL.—DODHIA. XLI.—BUHILA. XLII—SIKARWAL OR SIKARWAR. XLIII.—GOYAL. XLIV.—DEORA. XLV.—PARIA. XLVI.—PARIARIA. XLVII.—DHANDU XLVIII—DHANDAL OR DHONDAL. XLIX.—BORA. L.—BIDA. LI.—DETA. LII.—SINGARPAL. LIII.—KHIPA. LIV.—JASSOLIA. LV.—PHALSUNDIA. LVI.—SINMAL. LVII.—GOGADE. LVIII.—SAUDI. LIX.—JETANG. LX—BANDAR. LXI.—KASUMBLIA. LXII.—KARMOT. LXIII.—GAUR. LXIV.—PUAR LXV.—PUAR, PONWAR, OR PRAMARA. LXVI.—TAWAR. LXVII.—KELAN. LXVIII.—GOGLI. LXIX.—SUGAR. LXX.—MANGALIA. LXXI.—DHAWECHA. LXXII.—KALAEA. LXXIII.—KALAWAT. LXXIV.—UGA. LXXV.—SOR. LXXVI.—JASOR. LXXVII—SELOT. LXXVIII.—KALA. LXXIX.—BHARAKMAL. LXXX.—MAKWANA. LXXXI.—JHARECHA. LXXXII.—BARECHA. LXXXIII.—KOTECHA. LXXXIV.—KARWA. LXXXV.—BIRAWA. LXXXVI.—JAICHAND. LXXXVII.—KHAWARIA. LXXXVIII.—KARNOT. LXXXIX.—MAHECHA. XC.—TANWAR. XCI.—PARIHAR. XCII.—KHAIR. XCIII.—VIHIL, OR BIHIL. XCIV.—MAIPAWAT. XCV.—KABA. XCVI.—KHICHI. XCVII.—SONAGURRA. XCVIII.—PAWAICHA. XCIX.—BHURTA. C.—KALACHA. CI.—RAOKA. CII.—RANIKIA. CIII.—KHARURA. CIV.—TANTIA. CV.—INDAH. CVI.—SINDHIL. CVII.—KHORWA. CVIII.—DHOTI OR DHATI. CIX.—SONDIA OR SONDI. CX.—HADU. CXI.—RAJAWAT. CXII.—SUKHTAWAT. CXIII.—OR. CXIV.—RATHWA. CXV.—DUBIA. CXVI.—TONWAR. CXVII.—TAGARGARI. CXVIII.—MORI. CXIX.—BODANA.

XXX. Yâdu, Jâdu, or Jádon.

The Jâdu Rajpoots are the dominant tribe of Karauli, which State they have occupied from at least the tenth century, and probably from a much earlier period. The feudal aristocracy of that principality consists entirely of Jâdus. No other Rajpoots possess any rank whatever. They are an exceedingly illiterate people, very few being able to read and write. The Jâdus prefer the affix pâl, 'nourisher of cows,' to the more general Rajpoot affix of Singh, meaning lion. They are said to be brave fighting men, but bad cultivators. Wherever the Jadu "has to compete with cultivators of other castes on equal terms, he manifests his inferiority; and this is remarkably illustrated by the position of the Gonj, Khichri, and Panch Pir Thakurs in Karauli, who, being out of the caste, are not allowed the advantages enjoyed by respectable Jâdus, and are consequently on a lower level than Meenas and Gûjars"(a).

The principal divisions or *kotris* of the Karauli Jâdus are the following:—

The Principal Jâdu Clans.

1. Hâdoti. This clan usually supplies an heir to the sovereignty of Karauli on the failure of sons in the reigning family. Its chief bears the title of Rao. The original seat of the clan was the neighbouring village of Gareri, which was left for Hâdotî in 1697 in consequence of a dispute with the chief of Fathpur.

2. Amargarh. The first chief of Amargarh was Amar Mân, son of Raja Jago Mân.

3. Inâîti. The first chief of this clan was Bhûp Pâl, son of the Maharaja Chhatr Mân.

4. Râontra. The first chief of this clan was Bhoj Pâl.

5. Bartûn. The founder of this clan was Madan Mân, son of the Maharaja Mukund.

The five nobles representing the above five clans have forts of their own.

6. Hari Dâs. This clan has sixteen divisions, which lie on the western borders of the State.

7. Mukund. The Mukunds have eight divisions, their estates being situated to the north-east of the city (b).

Anjani is the patron goddess of the Jâdus. The ancestors of this race founded Jesalmere, in the year 1157. This city is the present capital of the Bhâtis.

The Jâdon Rajpoots of Karauli have a tradition that, in the year 1120, their ancestors erected the present fort at Dholpore. It is probable that they held lands in that territory in those days, but they must have been soon dispossessed, especially as we know that in 1194 Shahab-ud-din took possession of the kingdom of Kanauj, of which there is reason to believe that it formed a part.

The Jâdus have considerable possessions in Dholpore, in which State they own forty-nine villages. They have some families also in Dungarpore.

XXXI. Bhâti.

These Rajpoots are said to have established themselves on the Borwa hills of Merwara; and a tradition exists, that a Bhâtî Rajpoot, Ajit Singh, once bore the title of king of Merwara. They are strong to the west of the Bikaneer State, where they are divided into two great clans, namely:—

(a) Gazetteer of the Karauli State, by Captain P. W. Powlett, p. 18.
(b) *Ibid*, p 46.

The Bhâti Clans of Bikaneer.

1. The Raolot Clans—consisting of nine branches.
2. The Pugalia Clans—consisting of four branches.

These thirteen branches have their chief seats at Poogul, Rajasir, Ranair, Sutasir, Chakarra, Beechnok, Garrialah, Sûrjerah, Rundisir, Jangloo, Jaminsir, Kûdsû, and Naineah.

The Bhâtis of Bhatner are most probably Hindus, who have been converted to the Mahomedan faith. There is a colony of Bhâtis in Marwar, and another in Mallàni.

The Yâdu, Jâdu, or Jàdon Bhàti Rajpoots claim descent from the ancient Yâdu kings of the Lunar race The remote ancestors of the Bhàti Rajpoots came originally from Prayâg or Allahabad, whence they removed to Mathura, from which place, after remaining there for a long period, the tribe dispersed in various directions. The ruler of Jesalmere is of this tribe. The Bhàtis in former times subdued all the tracts south of the Garah; but their jurisdiction has been greatly diminished by the encroachments of the Ràthors. Some of the principal branches of the Bhâtis in Jesalmere are the following:—

Bhâti Clans of Jesalmere.

1. The Maldots.
2. The Kailans.
3. The Barsangs.
4. The Pohars.
5. The Tejmatahs.

The Maldots, says Tod, have the character of being the most daring robbers of the desert. They are descended from Rao Maldeo, and possess the fief of Baroo with eighteen villages. The chief seat of this tribe has been successively at Tumoli, Deorawal, and Jesalmere. Deorawal was founded by a Bhâti chief in the ninth century. He delighted in warfare, and consolidated the Bhâti rule in this barren region. So great were his exploits that he is regarded as the real founder of the tribe. The city and fort of Jesalmere were built in the middle of the twelfth century by Jesal, the sixth rajah in descent from Deoraj. About the year 1294 Alauddin sent an army against the Bhâtis, which destroyed the city of Jesalmere; but it was afterwards re-built. The Jesalmere princes continued independent for several centuries, and only submitted to the Mahomedans in the reign of Shah Jehan, under Rawal Sabal Singh, the twenty-fifth chief in succession to Jesal. The territory then was more extensive than in any other period of the nation's history, including Bhawalpore, extending northwards to the Sutlej, westward to the Indus, and eastwards and southwards embraced much of the tract subsequently added to Marwar and Bikaneer (*a*).

The Bhâtis of Marwar hold the chieftainships of Khejurla and Ahore.

The Bhâti, says Tod, "is not perhaps so athletic as the Râthor, or so tall as the Kachwâhâ, but generally fairer than either."

XXXII. Soda.

A small number of the Soda Rajpoots are in the Bikaneer State. and in Mallâni. This tribe is an offshoot of the Pramaras. In former times, they had possession of the whole of the great desert; and are still found scattered over it. The Umras and Sûmras, now Mahomedans, branches of the Sodas, established Umrakote, where Akbar was born, and Umrasomra. The ruler of Dhât, in the desert, is of this race (*b*). The Sodas have less prejudice than most Rajpoot tribes, and "will drink from the same vessel, and smoke out of the same hookah with a Mussulman, laying aside only the tube that touches the mouth." A Soda may always be known by the peculiarity of his turban.

In the extreme west of Rajputana, on the borders of Scinde, the Sodas display a singular blending of Hinduism and Islamism in their social customs and religious institutions. Their marriages are entirely in accordance with old Rajpoot customs, yet in their religion they conform, for the most part, to Mahomedan rites. Nevertheless, strange to say, they worshipped until very recently the gods of the Hindu pantheon.

XXXIII. Kachwâhâ.

This tribe has its principal seat at Jeypore, which State is mostly in the hands of Kachwâhâ chiefs. A branch of the tribe founded Amber in the tenth century, dispossessing the Meenas and Rajpoots, the former inhabitants of the country. One of the greatest princes of the Kachwâhâs of Jeypore was Rajah Maun Singh, a very distinguished general in the time of Akbar, whose reputation is still fresh among Rajpoot tribes. Another noted chief of the Jeypore family was Jai Singh II, commonly known as Siwai Jai Singh. It was he who erected observatories at Jeypore, Delhi, Benares, Mathura, and Ujain. That in Benares is, on the whole, in excellent preservation, and is an object of curiosity and interest to most European and American travellers visiting that city. This prince was the author of an important treaty between the chiefs of Jeypore, Jodhpore, and

(*a*) The Rajputana Gazetteer, Vol. II, pp. 170—72.

(*b*) Tod's Rajasthan—Madras Edition—Vol. I, p. 85.

Oodaipore, to resist the advancing influence of the Moghul rulers of India. It seems that the Sisodia chiefs of Oodaipore had in no single instance permitted alliances between their family and Moghul nobles, whereas both the Kachwâhâ and Râthor houses had repeatedly consented to such unions, whereby the purity of their Rajpoot blood had been seriously affected. This treaty, however, aimed at establishing a new bond of intercourse between the three tribes on the basis of electing the future chiefs of the two offending tribes from sons by Sisodia mothers and passing over elder sons by wives taken from other tribes. The treaty caused much dissatisfaction and strife, which eventually, instead of strengthening all these tribes, contributed greatly to their weakness (*a*).

In the twelfth century the Kachwâhâs were only great vassals of the Chauhân king of Delhi; and achieved their subsequent greatness with the aid of the Timoors. "Although the Kachwâhâs," observes Colonel Tod, "under their popular princes, as Pujûn, Rajah Mân, and the Mirza Rajah, have performed exploits as brilliant as any other tribes, yet they do not now enjoy the same reputation for courage as either the Râthors or the Hâras. This may be in part accounted for by the demoralization consequent on their proximity to the Moghul Court, and their participation in all its enervating vices; but still more from the degradations they have suffered from the Mahrattas, and to which their western brethren have been less exposed. Every feeling, patriotic or domestic, became corrupted wherever their pernicious influence prevailed" (*b*). "With a proper application of her (the State) revenues," remarks Tod in another place, "and princes like Rajah Mân to lead a brave vassalage, they would have foiled all the efforts of the Mahrattas; but their own follies and vices have been their ruin" (*c*). Most of the Rajpoots of Jeypore are Kachwâhâs, who may be divided into three classes, says Major Bayley, Political Agent of the State, namely, holders of estates, men in service, and cultivators. This last class is small, as Rajpoots are generally too proud to work in the fields, unless compelled by necessity (*d*).

The principal Kachwâhâ clans in the Jeypore State are twelve in number, and are the following:—

Kachwâhâ Clans of Jeypore.

1. Chatharbhojot—having the chieftainships of Pinar and Bhagrû.
2. Kallianot—having the chieftainship of Totwarra.

(*a*) The Rajputana Gazetteer, Vol. II, pp. 136, 137.
(*b*) Tod's Rajasthan—Madras Edition—Vol. II, p. 397.
(*c*) *Ibid*, p. 401.
(*d*) The Rajputana Gazetteer, Vol. II, p. 146.

3. Nathawat—with the chieftainship of Chomû.
4. Balbadharot—with the chieftainship of Acherol.
5. Khangarot—with the chieftainship of Thodrî.
6. Sûltanot—with the chieftainship of Chandsir.
7. Pachâenot—with the chieftainship of Sambra.
8. Gûgawat—with the chieftainship of Dhûnî.
9. Khûmbani—with the chieftainship of Bhanskho.
10. Khumbawat—with the chieftainship of Mahâr.
11. Shiubaranpota—with the chieftainship of Nîndir.
12. Banbîrpota—with the chieftainship of Batko.

The above are the Bârâh Kotrîs, or twelve great Kachwâhâ clans. In addition there are four other clans of the same tribe in the State. These are :—

13. Rajawat—with sixteen fiefs.

14. Narûka—having the chieftainship of Macherri. The chief of Uniârâ belongs to this clan, which has also a few representatives in Bhurtpore.

15. Bhankawat—with four fiefs.

16. Parinmalot—with one fief (*a*).

From the year 1037 A. D., when the Kachwâhâ Rajpoots having taken possession of this country made Amber their capital, down to 1728, Amber continued to be the royal city; but in the latter year the seat of power was transferred to the present city of Jeypore, which was founded by Siwai Jai Singh II.

In the Ajmere District, the Kachwâhâs are principally settled in the villages of Harmâra and Tilornia, in the extreme north of the district, and have *bhûmia* holdings in five villages. The ancestors of the chief of Harmâra narrowly escaped from losing their estates altogether. They were once partially seized by the Râhtors, and altogether by the Mahrattas. The British Government, however, has secured them to the family.

The Kachwâhâs of Bikaneer are divided into four classes, as follows :—

Kachwâhâ Clans of Bikaneer.

1. Girdharjîka.	3. Kachwâhâ.
2. Bhainrujîka.	4. Narûka.

The chief seat of the Kachwâhâs in Bikaneer is at Nynawas. The tribe has lands in Marwar and also in Bhurtpore.

About the middle of the last century, a Kachwâhâ seized a portion of the

(*a*) Tod's Rajasthan—Madras Edition—Vol. II. pp 403, 404.

Jeypore territory, and formed therefrom the principality of Ulwar, which exists to the present day. The tribe is found also in Dungarpore.

XXXIV. *Shekhawat.*

The Shekhawats are an offshoot of the Kachwâhâs of Jeypore, and are descended from Balo Ji, third son of the Raja of Udikarn, who became ruler of Jeypore in the year 1389. Balo Ji's grandson, Sheikh Ji, was so named in honour of a Mahomedan Sheikh, through whose prayers, it was believed, the child was born. The Sheikh ordained, says Tod, that, "at the birth of every Shekhawat male infant, a goat should be sacrificed, the *kalma* (Islamite creed) read, and the child sprinkled with the blood. Although four centuries have passed away since these obligations were contracted by Mokul (father of Sheikh Ji), they are still religiously maintained by the little nation of his descendants, occupying a space of ten thousand square miles. The wild hog, which, according to immemorial usage, should be eaten once a year by every Rajpoot, is rarely even hunted by a Shekhawat," out of respect to the memory of the Mahomedan saint (*a*). Balo Ji obtained Amrutsir as an appanage, which district was further increased by Sheikh Ji, so that his territory included three hundred and sixty villages, which in former times had been chiefly in the hands of Chauhân and Tuar tribes. The Shekhawats have the following clans:—

Shekhawat Clans.

1. The Bhojâni Clan.
2. The Sadhâni Clan—in the north of Shekhavati.
3. The Larkhâni Clan. This clan was formerly, says Tod, a community of robbers.
4. The Tajkhâni Clan.
5. Parsrâmpota Clan.
6. The Hurrâmpota Clan.
7. The Nathawat Clan. The chief houses of this clan are Samot and Chomû, the head having the title of Rawal.
8. The Raesilot Clan.

The Shekhawats are also settled in Mallâni, and in other parts of Rajputana.

About a hundred years ago, the Jeypore Government, being jealous of the growing power of the Shekhawatis, forcibly introduced the custom among them of the equal division of all real property among the sons on the death of their

(*a*) Tod's Rajasthan—Madras Edition—Vol. II, p. 359.

father. The result has been a general impoverishment and weakening of all the families of chiefs. Sîkar and Khetrî are the only districts exempt from the custom.

The principal chief of Shekhawati is Raja Ajit Singh, whose territory comprises the *pargannahs* of Khetrî, Bibai, Singhânâ, and Jhûnjnee. His revenue amounts to about three and-a-half lacs of rupees, of which he pays eighty thousand rupees as tribute to the Maharajah of Jeypore. Other dependencies in Shekhawati, which pay tribute to the same rule, are those of Sîkar, Baswa, Nawalgarh, Mandawâr, and Sûrajgarh (*a*). These chiefs govern their own territories with much independence, for although they acknowledge the suzerainty of the Maharajah of Jeypore, yet they are very jealous of any interference in their rule. At certain periods of the year they are obliged to appear at court, and to pay homage to the Jeypore Prince.

XXXV. Dewal.

A tribe in Marwar.

XXXVI. Solankhî, or Châlukya.

The Solankhis are in Jesalmere, Jhalawar, Bundee, Marwar, and Mallâni. The chief of Roopnagarh is of this tribe. His stronghold, says Tod, "commands one of the passes leading to Marwar." The Solankhîs are numerous in the State of Bundee, and a few are in Dungarpore.

XXXVII. Bhagela.

A branch of the Solankhîs. The Raja of Bhagelkhand, and the Raos of Peetapoor, Theraud, and Adaluj are of this tribe. Bhagela families are settled in Mallâni.

XXXVIII. Indar.

These are in Marwar and Mallâni.

XXXIX. Birpura.

A branch of the Solankhîs. The Rao of Lunawarra is of this tribe.

XL. Dodhia.

A tribe in Marwar.

XLI. Behila.

A branch of the Solankhis. The Rao of Kulianpoor, in Mewar, is of this tribe.

(*a*) The Rajputana Gazetteer, Vol. II, pp. 139, 40.

XLII. *Sikarwâl, or Sikarwâr.*

The small district of Sikarwar, on the right bank of the Chumbul, adjoining Jaduvati, is called after them. They live by cultivating the soil and the chase. There are clans of the tribe in Jeypore. In the small State of Dholpore the Sikarwârs are proprietors of twenty-three villages, and occupiers of eleven more.

XLIII. *Goyal.*

These are found in Marwar.

XLIV. *Deorâ.*

In Mallâni and Sirohi. They are a branch of the Chauhâns. The Rajpoot tribes of Mallâni are said to be fifty-two in number.

XLV. *Pariâ.*

In Mallâni.

XLVI. *Pariâria.*

In Mallâni.

XLVII. *Dhându.*

In Mallâni.

XLVIII. *Dhândal, or Dhondal.*

In Mallâni. Tod says, that the Dhondals are descended from Rao Gango, and are among the most ancient of the allodial chieftains of the desert.

XLIX. *Borâ.*

In Mallâni.

L. *Bidâ.*

In Mallâni.

LI. *Deta.*

In Mallâni.

LII. *Singarpâl.*

In Mallâni.

LIII. *Khipâ.*

In Mallâni.

LIV. *Jassolia.*

In Mallâni.

LV. *Phalsundia.*

In Mallâni.

LVI. *Sinmal.*

In Mallâni.

LVII. *Gogâde.*

In Mallâni.

LVIII. *Saudi.*

In Mallâni.

LIX. *Jetang.*

In Mallâni.

LX. *Bândâr.*

In Mallâni.

LXI. *Kasumblia.*

In Mallâni.

LXII. *Karmot.*

In Mallâni.

LXIII. Gaur.

The Gaurs are supposed to have come originally to Ajmere from Bengal, while performing a pilgrimage to the famous Dwarka Shrine under Raja Bachraj and Raja Bawan, in the time of Prithî Râja. The former, with his followers, settled in Ajmere, the latter at Kuchâman, in Marwar. Gradually the tribe gained possession of Junia, Sarwar, Deolia, and Srinagar; and in the reign of Akbar built for themselves Rajgarh. Notwithstanding the reverses to which they have been subjected, the city having been twice taken from them, once by the Râthors, and once by the Mahrattas, the Gaurs are still the owners of Rajgarh, and are occupiers of Kotaj, Danta, Jatia, and other places. They also took possession of Srinagar from the Powars, who have entirely left the district. The descendants of Raja Bawan have broad lands at Arjunpura, Tubeji, and elsewhere (*a*).

This tribe is also settled in Marwar. It has five branches or clans, namely, Outabir, Silhala, Tûr, Dûsena, and Bodano. In Ajmere the tribe possesses fourteen villages; and has a few families in Bundee.

LXIV. Tuâr.

The Tuârs are in Marwar; but their chief possessions, says Tod, are "the district of Tuârgar, on the right bank of the Chumbul, towards its junction with the Jumna; and the small chieftainship of Pâtun Tuârvati, or Torawati, in the Jeypore State, and whose head claims affinity with the ancient kings of Indraprastha" (*b*), that is, of Delhi. This small territory is to the north of Jeypore, between Kot Putti and Khetri. The Tuâr kings were expelled from Delhi about eight hundred years ago, on its capture by the Ghoris. The Tuârs of Malwa succeeded the Puârs, and reigned there one hundred and forty-two years, when they gave place to the Chauhâns.

LXV. Puâr, Powar, or Pramara.

These are located in Marwar, Jesalmere, and elsewhere. Although this tribe was once the most powerful of the Agnikulas, and founded great cities, ruling over wide tracts of country, yet little or nothing remains, except ruins, to illustrate its former splendour. The Puârs reigned over Malwa for upwards of a thousand years (*c*). The Rao of Bijolli, in Marwar, is of the ancient Pramaras of Dhâr, and belongs to the Maipawut branch of the tribe. The Pramaras of the

(*a*) Gazetteer of Ajmere-Merwara by Mr. J. D. Latouche. pp. 28 and 29.

(*b*) Tod's Rajasthan—Madras Edition — Vol. I. p. 80.

(*c*) For a detailed account of the Pramaras, see the Author's "Hindu Tribes and Castes," Vol. I. pp. 145 to 149.

plateau of Mewar, Tod remarks, are of the highest rank. The chief seat of the tribe in Bikaneer is at Jaitsisir.

The tribe has extensive possessions in Dholpore, where they are proprietors of no less than one hundred and three villages. It has also lands in Dungarpore.

LXVI. Tâwar, or Tânwar.

The Tâwars are in possession of two villages in Bikaneer. It has also some families in Marwar and Jesalmere.

LXVII. Kelan.
In Mallâni.

LXVIII. Gogli.
In Mallâni.

LXIX. Sugar.
In Mallâni.

LXX. Mângalia.
In Mallâni.

LXXI. Dhawecha.
In Mallâni.

LXXII. Kalâeâ.
In Mallâni.

LXXIII. Kalâwat.
In Mallâni.

LXXIV. Ugâ.
In Mallâni.

LXXV. Sor.
In Mallâni.

LXXVI. Jasor.
In Mallâni.

LXXVII. Selot.
In Mallâni.

LXXVIII. Kâlâ.
In Mallâni.

LXXIX. Bharakmal.
In Mallâni.

LXXX. Makwânâ.
In Mallâni.

LXXXI. Jharecha.
In Mallâni.

LXXXII. Barecha.
In Mallâni.

LXXXIII Kotecha.
In Mallâni.

LXXXIV. Karwa.
In Mallâni.

LXXXV. Birâwâ.
In Mallâni.

LXXXVI. Jaichand.
In Mallâni.

LXXXVII. Khâwaria.
In Mallâni.

LXXXVIII. Karnot.
In Mallâni.

LXXXIX. Mahecha.
In Mallâni.

XC. Tânwar.
In Jesalmere.

XCI. Parihâr.

In Jesalmere, and in most of the other States of Rajputana. The capital city of the tribe, in former times, was Mundawur, in Marwar; but they were dispossessed by the Râthors. The Parihârs have now no independent chieftainship in Rajputana. They have a colony, says Tod, "at the confluence of the Cohari, the Sinde, and the Chumbul, which has given its name to a commune of twenty-four villages besides hamlets situated amidst the ravines of these streams" (*a*). The tribe has also one village in Dholpore.

XCII. Khair.

A branch of the Pramaras. Their capital is Khyraloo.

(*a*) Tod's Rajasthan—Madras Edition—Vol. I, p. 92.

XCIII. *Vihil, or Bihil.*

A branch of the Pramaras. The heads of the tribe are chiefs of Chandravarti.

XCIV. *Maipawut.*

A branch of the Pramaras. The chief of Bijolli, in Mewar, is of this tribe.

XCV. *Kaba.*

A branch of the Pramaras. A few in Sirowi.

XCVI. *Khîchi.*

A branch of the Chauhâns, settled in Gagrown, Ragoogarh, Jesalmere, Boondi, Jhalawar, and elsewhere. They are descended from Manik Rae.

XCVII. *Sonagurra.*

A branch of the Chauhâns, in Jhalore, Marwar, and elsewhere.

XCVIII. *Pawaicha.*

A branch of the Chauhâns, settled in Pawagurh.

XCIX. *Bhûrta.*

A branch of the Solankhîs, in Jesalmere.

C. *Kalacha.*

A branch of the Solankhîs, in Jesalmere.

CI. *Raoka.*

A branch of the Solankhîs, settled in Thoda, Jeypore.

CII. *Ranikia.*

A branch of the Solankhîs, in Daisoori, Mewar.

CIII. *Kharura.*

A branch of the Solankhîs, in Allote and Jawura, Malwa.

CIV. *Tantia.*

A branch of the Solankhîs, in Chandbhur Sakunbari.

CV. *Indoh.*

A branch of the Parihârs, on the banks of the Loony.

CVI. *Sindhil.*

A branch of the Parihârs, on the banks of the Loony.

CVII. *Kâorwa.*

A nomadic tribe chiefly found in the Thul of Dhât. They move about with their cattle, encamping wherever water or pasturage is to be found.

CVIII. *Dhotî, or Dhâtî.*

A pastoral tribe at Dhât. They are a peaceable people, and in their habits resemble the Kâorwas.

CIX. *Sondia, or Sondî.*

These are numerous in the Chaumehla District of the Jhalawar State, where they amount to nearly twenty thousand persons, who are all agriculturists. These Rajpoots are a mixed race, probably descendants of outcasts. For many years they had a bad character as marauders. They were a terror to Sondwara. Before the peace of Mundesar they could muster a force of 1,249 horsemen and 9,250 footmen, all living on plunder. The Sondia has a fair countenance, wears a large white turban, and is readily recognized from all other Hindus. It is very common for Sondia women to marry a second time. These people are rude, robust, and profoundly ignorant. They are held in detestation by other tribes, and yet are greatly feared. All are addicted to the use of opium and to strong spirits, and both men and women are notoriously unrestrained in their sensual appetites. As they are much disunited among themselves, deeds of violence and bloodshed were formerly very common; but a great improvement has come over them in modern times (*a*).

CX. *Hadu.*

A tribe in Jhalawar.

CXI. *Rajawat.*

A tribe in Jhalawar.

CXII. *Sûkhtawât.*

A tribe in Jhalawar. The Sûkhtawât Rajpoots founded the *pargannah* of Awar, five hundred years ago.

CXIII. *Or.*

A Rajpoot tribe of workers in stone in the Jhalawar State. The great tank of Jhalrapatan is said to have been excavated by a Or Rajpoot named Jesu.

(*a*) Malcolm's Cential India, Vol. I.

CXIV. *Rathwa.*

A small tribe in Bundee.

CXV. *Dubia.*

A small tribe in Bundee.

CXVI. *Tonwâr.*

This tribe is said to be the first of the Rajpoot tribes which established itself in Dholpore, whither they came, it is supposed, in the beginning of the eleventh century. They are now chiefly to be found in the Rahna Division of Rajakhera. The tribe is in possession of fifteen villages. It has also some families in Dungarpore.

CXVII. *Tagargari.*

A tribe in Dholpore, where it is the proprietor of half a dozen villages.

CXVIII. *Mori.*

The tribe has three villages in Dholpore.

CXIX. *Bodana.*

A tribe settled in Dungarpore.

CHAPTER V.

CASTES.

THE VAISYA CASTES: MERCHANTS, BANKERS, AND TRADERS. THE KAYASTHS. BARDS AND GENEALOGISTS. GOLDSMITHS AND JEWELLERS. AGRICULTURAL TRIBES AND CASTES. HERDSMEN, SHEPHERDS, AND REARERS OF CAMELS. SMALL TRADERS. MANUFACTURERS OF BEADS BANGLES AND VARIOUS ARTICLES. WEAVERS AND DYERS, &c. PHYSICIANS AND SURGEONS. BLACKSMITHS, BRAZIERS, MASONS, CARPENTERS, TINKERS. POTTERS, DIGGERS, &c. DEVOTEES, RELIGIOUS MENDICANTS. SERVANTS AND PERSONAL ATTENDANTS. JUGGLERS, ACROBATS, SNAKE-CHARMERS, BUFFOONS, DRUM-BEATERS. FOWLERS AND HUNTERS. WORKERS IN LEATHER. THIEVES, ROBBERS, AND WATCHMEN. SCAVENGERS AND OTHER LOW CASTES.

THE VAISYA: MERCHANTS, BANKERS, AND TRADERS.

The trading class is found more or less in all the States. They are divided into numerous branches. Bankers and merchants are mostly Jains, the small traders being generally Hindus.

1. *The Agarwálas.*

One of the principal trading castes of Ajmere, Marwar, Bikaneer, Mallâni, Jesalmere, Bhurtpore, and Bundee.

They are largely attached to the Jain religion, and are generally wealthy. In Bikaneer the Agarwâlas are the principal traders in English imported goods. They are prosperous in Karauli, and to some extent cultivate the soil.

2. *The Oswâls.*

A leading trading caste in Ajmere, Jesalmere, Marwar, Bhurtpore, Bundee, Dungarpore, and Bikaneer, who, it is said, sprang from Osanaggri, near the Lûni, in Marwar. Like the Agarwâlas, they are chiefly Jains, and are generally well off. The Oswâls have the following clans in Bikaneer:—

1. Dada.
2. Kotári.
3. Sethia.
4. Sirono.
5. Sawan Súkha.
6. Abani.
7. Bhantia.
8. Goleha.

The following are important clans of the Oswâls of Marwar:—

1. Bhandári.
2. Mohnot.
3. Singwi.
4. Muhta.
5. Lodha.

Members of these clans have held very high offices in the State of Marwar. Most of the Oswâls of Mallâni are cultivators.

3. *The Maheshwarîs.*

Traders in Ajmere, Jesalmere, Mallâni, Bhurtpore, Bundee, Marwar, and Bikaneer. In the latter territory the Maheshwarîs and Oswâls are the richest Banyas. They are opium traders, contractors, bankers, and the like, and their business is generally far from home. The following are subdivisions of this tribe :—

1. Daga.	5. Bâgri.	9. Mundra.
2. Pugali.	6. Lada.	10. Kotâri.
3. Damâni.	7. Mohota.	11. Râti.
4. Mintri.	8. Sadhani.	

At the marriage ceremony of Maheshwarîs as well as Pancholis, when the bridegroom enters the bride's house, her maternal uncle lifting her up carries her in his arms seven times round the bridegroom.

4. *The Bijaburjis.*

Traders in Ajmere.

5. *The Khandelwals.*

Traders in Ajmere.

6. *The Dhûsars.*

Traders in Ajmere and Bhurtpore.

7. *The Saraogîs.*

These flourish in Karauli, where they belong to the Jain religion Some of them are cultivators. They are also in Marwar and Bhurtpore.

8. *The Srî Mâls.*

Traders in Karauli, attached to the Jain religion. They are settled also in Marwar and Bhurtpore.

9. *The Palliwâls.*

Jain traders in Karauli, Bhurtpore, Dungarpore, and elsewhere. They came originally from Palli.

10. *The Porwâls.*

Traders in Marwar.

11. *The Sri-sri-mâls.*

Traders in Marwar.

12. *The Vijawargis.*

Traders in Marwar.

13. *The Bhattias.*

Traders in Jesalmere and in the Rajputana desert. They are Rajpoots, who have degraded themselves from their original position. Their habits are like those of the Arorahs.

14. *The Lohanas.*

A numerous tribe of traders and writers in Dhât and Talpoora. They are said to have been originally Rajpoots. Many pursue various callings.

15. *The Arorahs.*

A tribe in the Rajputana desert, addicted to agriculture, trade, and many other pursuits.

16. *Bohra.*

Traders in tin, iron, and other wares.

17. *Khondehwal.*

A trading class in Bhurtpore.

18. *Mahor.*

Traders in Bhurtpore.

19. *Dilwaria.*

Traders in Bhurtpore.

20. *Khestri.*

Traders in Bhurtpore.

21. *Nogdra.*

Traders in Dungarpore.

22. *Narsinghpura.*

Traders in Dungarpore.

23. *Bhutera.*

Traders in Dungarpore.

24. *The Khatris.*

The Khatris are found in the north parts of Bikaneer and in Marwar, and in other parts of Rajputana.

They are chiefly bankers and traders. A few cultivate land. In Mallâni the Khatris stamp dyed stuffs ; and those who work for chiefs at this trade are exempt from the payment of taxes. Several clans of Khatris hold estates in Jeypore.

THE KAYASTHS.

There are three clans of Kayasths in Ajmere, some members of which wear the sacred cord. These acknowledge no mutual relationship, and hold no social intercourse with one another. They are as follows :—

1. Ajmere. 2. Ramsar. 3. Kekri.

The Kayasths are accountants and revenue officials over villages and districts. They hold estates free from revenue, and have been hereditary *kanungoes* from the time of the Moghul emperors. The local name for Kayasths in Marwar is Pancholi.

There is a branch of them also in Jhalawar.

The Kayasths of Bhurtpore have the following subdivisions :—

1. Mathur.	5. Suratdhaj.	9. Balmik.
2. Bhatnagar.	6. Amisht.	10. Aithana.
3. Sri Basta.	7. Gaur.	11. Kulshrista.
4. Sakseina.	8. Karan.	12. Nigaen.

The two first of these clans only are found in the Bundee State, each of which is divided into two branches, which do not intermarry.

BARDS AND GENEALOGISTS.

The Châran Tribe.

The Chârans are a people of great respectability and influence in Rajputana. They are the national bards, which is their chief and most important vocation, especially as attached to great Rajpoot families, whose praises they sing, and whose pedigrees they rehearse. They also perform a number of miscellaneous duties in connection with their high office. The Chârans possess a good many villages in some States. They are a sacred race, and possess many privileges in virtue of their position. In Marwar they hold large grants of land, which have been given to them from religious motives, and for the same reasons enjoy certain immunities as traders (*a*).

The Tirwâris are a kind of Châran in Marwar. The two principal clans of the tribe in that State are :—

1. Bânkedâs.	2. The Chaendâs.

These clans "hold the post of bard; and it is their duty to collect and preserve the records of each reigning chief, and embody them in their histories, which is done both in prose and verse. They also compose odes commemorative of the most important passing events, which they recite before the Maharaja in Durbar. They receive rich gifts from the chiefs of the courts to which they belong; and the highest honors are paid to them" (*b*).

A singular and very bad custom prevails among the Chârans of Marwar, of a young man and young woman, when betrothed, eating opium together.

In Mallâni there are two clans of Chârans, namely :—

1. Barath Chârans.	2. Garwi Chârans.

(*a*) Gazetteer of Marwar, by Major C. K. M. Walter, p. 23.

(*b*) *Ibid*, p. 30.

There is a tradition that the Barath Chârans were originally Bhâti Rajpoots. The village of Durmara, in Nagor, is held by the Barath Chârans in *udak*, or rent-free. They worship chiefly Mâthwiji. The Garwi Chârans came originally from Kachh. They are great traders, and do not receive alms like the Baraths. The two clans do not intermarry, or eat and smoke together. Both classes of Chârans consider themselves to be above the law, and pay no dues. Resenting all interference with themselves, they readily commit *chândi* if not left alone, that is, they wound their persons with sharp knives and daggers, and even kill themselves. The Garwi Chârans have always been much respected, and in times of national feud and disturbance have been free from molestation wherever they went.

In Bikaneer an image erected to Karniji, the Châran woman through whose agency it is supposed the State came into the hands of Bika and his descendants, is the chief object of worship, and her shrine is the principal one in Bikaneer.

The Chârans of Central India are divided into two branches :—

1. Kachili.	2. Maru.

The former of these are horse and camel dealers ; but the latter are devoted to the special duties of the tribe.

The Bhât Tribe.

In the North-Western Provinces, Bhâts and Chârans are frequently one and the same tribe ; but in Rajputana they are separate tribes with separate duties. The Bhâts are genealogists, and concern themselves about the pedigrees of great families. They also engage in trade. The tribe has great influence in all the native States, and is held in great awe by the other tribes, in the same way as the Chârans. They possess rent-free estates, and receive presents at weddings.

The Chârans and Bhâts are the chief carriers in the State of Marwar. "Their sacred character," says Tod, "overawes the lawless Rajpoot chief ; and even the savage Kali and Bheel, and the plundering Sahrae of the desert, dread the anathema of these singular races, who conduct the caravans through the wildest and most desolate regions" (*a*). Both these tribes are carriers and traders with pack-bullocks in the State of Bundee.

The Bhâts of Bhurtpore are few in number, and have three branches, namely :—

1. Suth.	2. Bandi.	3. Mangal.

In Bundee, the Bhâts perform the duties of marriage negotiators and reciters of genealogical history at public festivals.

(*a*) Tod's Rajasthan—Madras Edition— Vol. I, p. 602.

GOLDSMITHS AND JEWELLERS.

The Sonârs.

These work in gold, silver, brass, and other metals. In Mallâni they also pursue agriculture. In that State they are divided into two branches,—the Sonârs, and the Mer Sonârs. These do not intermarry, or eat and drink together. They are found in several of the States.

AGRICULTURAL TRIBES AND CASTES.

Lodha.

Cultivators of extensive lands in the eastern districts of Rajputana. In Dholpore they are proprietors of forty-five villages, are occupiers of ninety-one more, and in addition are cultivators of nearly seventeen thousand acres of land.

Mâli.

The Mâlis number upwards of eleven thousand persons in Ajmere, and are good cultivators. They occupy the greater portion of Kusbah, Ajmere, and are scattered about the Rajputana States. They are a very industrious people, and are found in considerable numbers in the eastern districts.

Kâchî.

Laborious cultivators in Rajputana as in other parts of India. They are numerous in the eastern districts, where their lands are extensive. In Dholpore they have a community of fifteen thousand persons, who cultivate nearly twenty thousand acres of land.

Kumbi, or Kurmi.

Cultivators, who are found especially to the south of the Arvalis, having come originally from Central and Southern India. The agriculturists of Dungarpore are chiefly Kurmis.

Kir.

A small tribe in Ajmere, whose employment is the cultivation of melons.

Sirwi.

A class of cultivators in Marwar.

Kalbi.

Cultivators in Mallâni, on estates bordering on the Lûni. They are worshippers of Vishnu.

Pithil.

The principal agriculturists of the desert in Rajputana.

Kirâr.

Landholders and agriculturists in Jeypore, Jhalawar, and other States. Some of them hold large estates.

Bishnawi.

Cultivators in the district of Chahotan in Mallâni.

Mehwâti.

Cultivators in Jhalawar.

Dhâkar.

Cultivators in Jhalawar.

HERDSMEN, SHEPHERDS, AND REARERS OF CAMELS.

Ahir.

Herdsmen and cultivators, especially in the eastern districts, where they possess extensive lands. In Bhurtpore some Ahirs pursue the occupation of coachmen.

Godariya, or Garariya.

Shepherds.

Rebari.

These are properly breeders of camels, but are also growers of rice. They form a small community in Ajmere. In Mallâni the Rebaris keep large herds of sheep and goats as well as cattle and camels. The tribe is scattered about various parts of the Rajputana desert. In Bhurtpore they are cultivators as well as camel-drivers.

SMALL TRADERS.

Tamboli.

Pawn and betelnut-sellers.

Teli.

Oil-crushers and oil-sellers in Ajmere and other districts.

Ghosi.

Milk and butter sellers of Ajmere.

Burbhûnja, or Bhurji.

Grain roasters.

Kulâl.

Spirit-sellers.

Sungâ.

Distillers of spirits in Mallâni, where they style themselves first class traders.

Bisâti.

Pedlars

MANUFACTURERS OF BEADS AND VARIOUS ARTICLES, WEAVERS, DYERS, &c.

Munihar.

Manufacturers of bangles or armlets.

Lakhera.

Bangle-makers and dealers in lac or sealing-wax. They pay no taxes, but have to repair the bangles of the chief's family.

Odi.

In Jesalmere.

Gwariâ.

Rope-makers in Marwar.

Rangrez.

Dyers.

Chîpî.

Markers of chintz and other fabrics in Ajmere, Jhalawar, and elsewhere.

Patwâ.

Braiders and artizans.

Julaha.

Weavers.

Dabgar.

Manufacturers of leathern jars for holding *ghi*, or clarified butter.

Ghânchâ.

Basket-makers in Marwar. In Mallâni they are oilmen and cultivators.

Koli.

In the States of Karauli, Bhurtpore, and Dholpore, the Kolis are an important class of weavers. They are a low caste race, eaters of the flesh of cows and of carrion, and are consequently regarded with abhorrence by respectable tribes.

The Koli tribes are numerous in the Rajputana desert, where they assume appellations, such as Chauhân Koli, Râthor Koli, Parihâr Koli, and the like, showing their illegitimate descent from Rajpoots and aboriginal Kolis. Their habits are very low. Many are engaged in agriculture.

PHYSICIANS AND SURGEONS.

Baid.

Native physicians. In some places they hold hereditary State pensions.

Bâgri.

In Mallâni they are cattle doctors. They also operate on the human body in cases of lithotomy.

BLACKSMITHS, BRAZIERS, MASONS, CARPENTERS, TINKERS.

Lohâr.

Blacksmiths, distributed in small numbers throughout the States. The Lohârs of Bundee extract iron from the ore by smelting.

Sikligar.

Sharpeners of steel and iron implements, cutlers, knife-grinders.

Thathera.

Braziers.

Râj, or Râjkumhar.

Masons.

Khâti.

Carpenters, and village servants, in Ajmere and other States.

Silâwat.

Stone-masons, builders, and also cultivators. They intermarry with the Khâtis.

Sangtarâsh.

Stone-cutters.

Kalaigar.

Tinkers.

POTTERS, DIGGERS, &c.

Kumhâr.

Potters. The chief custom at the marriage ceremony of the Jâtias of this tribe, is for a thread to be bound round the bride's wrist; which, among most other castes, on exchange of raw sugar and cocoanuts, confirms the betrothal of the parties.

The caste is divided into three great branches, namely :—

1.—The Karsâs, who are cultivators exclusively.

2.—These are potters and cultivators.

3.—Jâtia Kumhârs, called Jâts in Mallâni, workers in wood, rope-makers, and thread-twisters, and also cultivators. The Jâtias do not intermarry with the other two classes. The native chiefs of Mallâni absolve the Kumhârs, when cultivators, from the cultivator's tax of three rupees, and in return are supplied with earthen vessels. They are also excused from the payment of the house-tax of one rupee, and also of the fee paid by all agriculturists on the marriage of their (the Kumhârs') daughters.

There are upwards of eight thousand Kumhârs in Ajmere and Merwara, and between two and three thousand in Dholpore.

Khârwâl.

Men employed on the saltworks of Marwar.

Beldar.

Diggers of tanks and wells.

DEVOTEES, RELIGIOUS MENDICANTS.

The Gosains.

These are professedly devotees. Some are celibates, others marry. They eat flesh, drink spirits, worship Shiva, and at death are buried, some in a sitting posture, others at full length. Many, especially the celibates, subsist on charity. The married Gosains work for their living by cultivating the fields. The tribe has twelve subdivisions in Rajputana, ten of which are found in Mallâni, namely :—

1. Giri.	4. Ban.	7. Parit.
2. Puri.	5. Saraswati.	8. Parghat.
3. Bhârti.	6. Sâgar.	9. Arun.

10. Runkhar.

The Nâths.

Many persons of this caste, especially those in good circumstances, do not marry. These bear the appellation of Nihang. The Nâths are easily recognized by the stone ornament which they wear in the lobes of their ears.

The Nâgas.

Sects of military devotees attached to the various sects, some of whom are employed as soldiers in the native armies of Rajputana. They are vowed to celibacy and to arms, and constitute a sort of military order. They are separated into several sects, as follows :—

The Nâga Sects.

1. Dâdapanthi.	2. Râmnathi.	3. Vishnu Swâmi.

The first sect consists of followers of Dâdu Panth, and the second of followers of Râm Nâth. These sects are replenished by children placed under their charge as disciples by their parents.

Khâki.

Religious mendicants, who go about almost naked, having only a thick cord round their loins, their bodies being smeared with ashes.

Râm Sanehi.

This sect has its head-quarters at Shâhpura. Its members worship no images, and are influenced by love for Râm, as their designation indicates. They wander about in pairs, and are very lightly clothed.

Kabirpanthi.

A sect well known in Northern India, having a few members in Bundee and elsewhere in Rajputana.

Desântari.

A class of beggars in Mallâni. If any Hindu festival happens to fall on an unlucky Saturday, valuable presents are made to the Desântaris, in order to dispel the evil omen, in return for which they worship the God Saturn. They also receive all alms given on a Saturday.

Motesar.

A tribe of beggars peculiar to Marwar. They receive gifts at marriages from Chârans and Bhâts, or through their instrumentality.

SERVANTS AND PERSONAL ATTENDANTS.

Bâri.

A people found in many parts of the North-Western Provinces as well as in Rajputana. They make plates or cups of leaves, stitched together with little wooden pegs, for the purpose of holding food: The Bâris also act the part of servants in respectable Hindu families.

A curious custom prevails in Marwar on the birth of an heir to the throne. An impression of the child's foot is taken by a Bâri on cloth covered with saffron, and is exhibited to the native chiefs, who reward the Bâri liberally for the sight. The Kishnagur chief returns the compliment on the birth of an heir in his family.

Mehra, or Kahâr.

These are in Marwar, Ajmere, Bhurtpore, and elsewhere. They are bearers, palankeen-carriers, water-carriers, day-labourers, and servants. Their occupation seems to differ somewhat in various States.

Chobdâr.

Silver-stick bearers in waiting; messengers.

Jâti.

Schoolmasters in Mallâni, who are attached to the Jain religion.

Gûrûra.

Spiritual teachers of the Megwâls. They are also cultivators and teachers.

Nâi.

Barbers. Their wives are nurses and wetnurses in Ajmere and elsewhere. The Nâis discharge important duties in the houses of the native chiefs. They enjoy certain special privileges.

Bulâhi.

Messengers and grooms. This tribe numbers twenty-three thousand in Ajmere and Merwara. It has four villages in Beawar.

Darzî.

Tailors.

Dhobi.

Washermen. It would be interesting to know their subdivisions in the several States. They are allowed special privileges granted to some other castes.

JUGGLERS, ACROBATS, SNAKE-CHARMERS, BUFFOONS, DRUM-BEATERS.

Dholi.

Beaters of drums, who are paid by the villagers either in food or clothing, or both, and who receive various other presents.

Jâgri.

Beaters of small drums at dances and festivals.

Nat.

Acrobats, jugglers, and gipsies.

Santhia.

A wandering tribe of Jhalawar.

Kanjar.

Snake-charmers ; a wandering tribe.

Râwal.

Buffoons in Marwar.

FOWLERS AND HUNTERS.

Chiremâr.

Bird-catchers.

Shikâri.

Hunters.

WORKERS IN LEATHER.

Chamâr.

Labourers, tanners, workers in leather, cultivators, and so forth.

These are numerous in some parts of Rajputana, especially in the eastern districts. In Bikaneer they are also called Balâi. Nearly fifty years ago a Chamâr, named Lâlgir, founded a religious sect in that State, to which high officials, Rajpoots, and others have attached themselves. His tenets, which are still those of the sect, are the following :—" He denounced idolatry, and taught his followers to call on the incomprehensible (Alak); and his sole worship consisted in crying 'Alak, Alak!' Charity was to be practised; the taking of life and meat as food was forbidden; asceticism was held profitable to subdue passion; and the sole reward was attainment in this life to purity, untroubled contemplation, and serenity. There was no future state. Heaven and hell (that is, happiness or misery) were within, and may be made independent of external circumstances; but all perishes with the body, which is finally resolved into the elements; and man has no immortal part. Peace in life, and a good name after it, were the sole, but sufficient, inducements to the practice of virtue' (*a*).

The Chamârs are properly workers and dealers in leather; but they are also agriculturists. They likewise perform various menial duties for their employers. In Karauli they often get a certain share in each crop, and certain perquisites, for their labours.

The Gûrûra is the priest of the Chamârs in Marwar. In the State of Dholepore the Chamârs number upwards of thirty-two thousand persons, eighteen thousands of whom cultivate nearly twenty thousand acres of land.

(*a*) Gazetteer of the Bikanîr State, by Captain P. W. Powlett. Political Agent, Ulwar. p. 91.

Megwâl.

In Mallâni the tribe is divided into three clans, which can eat together, but not intermarry. They are said to perform the general work of a village in looking after travellers and so forth, and therefore, although of low caste, are of much importance publicly.

1. The Bâmbis. These are said to be the same caste as the Chamârs of the North-Western Provinces. They are workers in leather, weavers, and village servants; and receive the skins of all unclaimed dead animals.

2. The Jâtias. These are the same as Regars elsewhere. Their special occupation is that of dyeing, and of working in untanned leather. They eat the flesh of dead animals.

3. The Bangâras. Cloth manufacturers and cultivators.

The Megwâls of Jesalmere manufacture blankets of sheep's wool, and weave cloth.

Sargarâ.

A kind of Chamâr. They are cultivators and drum-beaters.

Sanjogi Shami.

The offspring of parents of different castes, an ex-communicated race, regarded with much disfavor by Hindus. In Mallâni these persons are cultivators and beggars.

Mochi.

Shoe-makers and workers in leather. "The Thakurs only pay half price for their shoes, some nothing at all; and the Mochis are allowed to cultivate as much land as they can by their own household rent-free." If the Mochis have no lands, they are recompensed in some other way.

Regar.

They are supposed to correspond with the Chamârs of the North-Western Provinces.

Dhanak.

Swineherds and grooms.

Khatik.

Tanners and grooms.

THIEVES, ROBBERS, AND WATCHMEN.

Thori, or Thaori.

A tribe in Ajmere, the Lakhi jungle; and Rajputana desert. They were once notorious robbers.

Chûra.

A tribe in Mewar and the Rajputana desert. They are attached to many chiefs as servants. They guard the barriers of the Rajputana desert. They were once notorious robbers.

Sânsi.

Another class of thieves in Ajmere and other States.

Bâuria and Moghya.

A caste of thieves and robbers in Marwar and elsewhere, professing, like other low tribes in Rajputana, to be descended from Rajpoots. They are employed as village watchmen, but are also well-known professional thieves. These people are styled Bâuria to the north of the Arvali Range, and Moghya to the south. Their villages are on the confines of Tonk, Meywar, and Gwalior, as well as in Nimbahera, Neemuch, and Marwar. They eat flesh and drink spirits.

SCAVENGERS AND OTHER LOW CASTES

Khâkrob, or Khabrûk.

A sweeper caste in Jesalmere.

Bhangi.

A tribe in Ajmere, Bhurtpore, and elsewhere. The sweeper caste, which has numerous representatives throughout the North-Western Provinces.

Dom.

One of the lowest of the outcast tribes in Rajputana as elsewhere. In the Karauli State the Dom is a marriage negotiator, and gets four seers, or eight pounds, of grain for every marriage performed, as well as ten pounds from every crop grown in connexion with every house in a village.

Baid.

A low people of Marwar.

Satia.

An outcast tribe of Marwar.

Dhânkâ.

The Dhânkâs are a low caste in Marwar.

CHAPTER VI.

THE MAIR, OR MER TRIBES.

I.—THE CHAUHAN MAIRS: 1, THE CHITA TRIBES; 2, THE BARAR TRIBES. II.—THE PRAMAR MAIRS. III.—THE MOTI MAIRS. IV.—THE DAKUL MAIRS. V.—THE GAHLOT MAIRS. VI.—THE PATALIYAT MAIRS. VII.—THE CHAUROT MAIRS. VIII.—THE BHARSAL MAIRS. IX.—THE BUCH MAIRS. X.—THE KHARWAL MAIRS. XI—THE MAMNOT MAIRS XII.—THE SELOT MAIRS. XIII.—THE BANAT MAIRS. XIV.—THE BANNA MAIRS.

These tribes are the principal inhabitants of Mairwara, or Merwara, from whom the country derives its name. Although they are not supposed to be an aboriginal race, yet they have occupied this tract for a very long period, notwithstanding many efforts to subjugate them. The Mahomedan emperors failed to bring them under their sway. The primitive inhabitants were probably fugitives from other parts of India, who, taking advantage of the impenetrable forests of Merwara, made them their abode. The word 'Mer' means 'hill'; so that the Mairs are in reality hillmen. Mr. LaTouche states that the word 'Mer' or 'Mair' designates not so much a distinct caste or tribe as the inhabitants generally of this portion of the Arvali Range. It is singular, however, if this be the case, that they should be regarded as a separate people.

The Mairs have a bad reputation of being a very dirty people. This may arise from their living in a hilly region, for it is a singular circumstance that all the hill tribes in India are a filthy race. As Hindus, the Mairs are extremely lax, and think little of the orthodox deities worshipped elsewhere. They pay great veneration to the Mâkutji and Goramji hills, and hold a yearly festival in honour of Mâta, or the goddess of smallpox.

On occasion of the great Holi festival, a game called Abera is played in every village on the first and last day. It is thus described :—" The whole village turns out into the jungle, each man armed with two sticks, about a yard long, called *pokhri*. Opium and tobacco are provided by the headmen. Having formed a line, the people commence beating for hares and deer, knocking them over by a general discharge of sticks as they start up. A number of hares are killed in this way. If the *mahajans*, or bankers, will pay—and the *mahajans* of Ajmere and Merwara, being Jains, are exceedingly tender of life—the people will not kill on the second day. The festival of the Holi concludes with a game like 'touch in the ring.' The people consume a good deal of tobacco, but very little opium. Tobacco they carry in an oval wooden box called *ghata*, and the principal men append a long wooden handle to this box, which they always carry about with them. The handle signifies that all who ask will get tobacco" (*a*).

Although regarding themselves as Hindus, they are but little affected by strict Hindu usages. They will eat the flesh of most animals, including cows, which all Hindus proper regard as sacred. Even Brahmans in this heterodox State will eat flesh. The people generally are addicted to hero-worship. It is said that at one time they used to sacrifice their first-born sons to Mâtâ, the goddess of smallpox, a disease occasionally very prevalent in Merwara. It is still customary to sacrifice a buffalo on the birth of the first son in a family.

I.—The Chauhân Mair Tribes.

The two chief tribes of Mairs, like many other tribes in Northern India, trace their descent from Prithi Raja, the famous Chauhân king; and their traditions state, that a son of Prithi Raja, named Jodh Lâkhun, married a girl of the Meena tribe, "who had been seized in a marauding expedition near Bundee, supposing her to be a Rajpootani. When he discovered his mistake, he turned away the mother and her two sons, Anhal and Anup. The exiles wandered to Chang, in Beawar, where they were hospitably entertained by the Gujars of that place. Anhal and Anup rested one day under a Bar, or fig-tree; and prayed that, if it was destined that their race should continue, the trunk of the tree might be rent in twain. The instant occurrence of the miracle raised them from their despondency; and the splitting of the fig-tree is a cardinal event in the history of the race, according to the following distich:—

Charar se Chîta bhayo, aur Barar bhayo Bar ghât
Shâkh ek se do bhaye; jagat bakhânî jât.

"The meaning of which is, 'from the sound "charar" (the splitting *noise*) the Chîtas are called, and the Barârs from the splitting *itself* of the fig-tree. Both are descended from one stock. The world has made these tribes famous'" (*b*). From this tradition respecting the origin of the Chauhân Mairs it is plain, if there be any truth in it, that they are partly the offspring of Rajpoots, and partly of Meenas.

(*a*) Rajputana Gazetteer, Vol. II, p. 47.
(*b*) Gazetteer of Ajmere-Merwara, by Mr. J. D. LaTouche, p. 34.

While there are several minor tribes, the Chauhân Mairs are chiefly divided into two principal tribes, the Chîtas and the Barârs, each having twenty-four *gotras*, or class subdivisions. The Mers have fifty-one villages in Ajmere, two hundred and forty-one in Beawar, and eighty-eight in Todgarh (*a*).

1.—*The Chita Tribe of Chauhân Mairs.*

These first settled at Chang, to the north-west of Merwara, and after a time destroyed or expelled the Gujars, the former occupants. Gradually they took possession of all the most important towns and villages of Merwara, and built others, such as Jâk, Shamgarh, Lulna, Hattûn, Kûkra, Kot Kirana, and Naî. The Chîtas became the ruling class in the district, and held in subjection at one time as many as sixteen other Mer tribes, from whom they received as tribute one-fourth of the produce of the soil, and of all plundering expeditions (*b*). They are powerful and wealthy, and possess one hundred and seventeen villages in Beawar, sixteen in Todgarh, besides portions of many others.

Some of the principal Chîta *gotras* or clans are the following :—

(1.) *The Merât Clan.*

This clan is the chief of the twenty-four. Its members are partly Mahomedans. They sprang from Mera, who flourished about two hundred and fifty years ago. They are divided into two great branches, the Kâtâts and the Gorâts.

i. *The Kâtâts.*

Their ancestor was Harâj, grandson of Mera, about whom the following tale is told :—During a night of terrific rain, Harâj, who was a soldier in the army of Aurungzebe, the emperor of Delhi, remained firm at his post as sentry, with his shield over his head. When the Emperor heard of the circumstance, he exclaimed : "In the Marwar tongue they call a brave soldier Kâtâ ; let this man be henceforth called Kâtâ" (*c*). The Kâtât Merâts are powerful, enterprising, and numerous. They occupy seventy-eight villages in Beawar, and nine in Ajmere, where they have formed for themselves new *gotras*, the Bahâdur Khâni being the most influential. The chief Kâtâts of Hattun Châng and Jâk, in Beawar, are styled Khans, a Mahomedan title, while those elsewhere bear the common Hindu designation of Thâkur. The Kâtâts are a very degenerate kind of Mahomedans.

It is to be regretted that the Kâtâts of Ajmere are beginning to observe some

(*a*) Gazetteer of Ajmere-Merwara, by Mr. J. D. LaTouche, p. 34.

(*b*) *Ibid.*

(*c*) *Ibid*, p. 35.

of the pernicious customs of Mahomedans, especially that of the seclusion of their women, while in Merwara the Kâtât women have the same freedom as the men.

ii. *The Gorâts.*

These are descendants of Gora, a brother of Harâj, and are Hindus. They have spread southwards, and have twenty-one villages in Beawar, Kalinjar and Kabra being the chief of them, thirteen in Todgarh, and one in Ajmere.

The Kâtâts and Gorâts, although belonging to different religions, will eat together all kinds of food.

(2.) *The Laget Clan.*

The Lagets hold six villages in Beawar.

(3.) *The Nanset Clan.*

They possess Bargaon, Palran, Pharkia, Manpura, and Hathibata, in Ajmere, besides lands in other villages.

(4.) *The Rajoriya Clan.*

These hold three villages in Beawar.

(5.) *The Bedariyat Clan.*

This clan has three villages in Ajmere.

(6.) *The Bajriyat Borwara Clan.*

(7.) *The Biladiya Clan.*

(8.) *The Pithrot Clan.*

(9.) *The Balot Clan.*

(10.) *The Nadot Clan.*

The remaining clans are spread over Merwara (*a.*)

2.—*The Barâr Tribe of Chauhân Mairs.*

These are descended from Anup, brother of Anhal. They are only to be found in Merwara. The tribe occupies eleven villages in Beawar, and forty-eight in Todgarh, including the whole of the southern part of this district. "They are more unsophisticated, honest, and straightforward than the Chîtas. They call themselves Râwat, a petty title of nobility; and would be insulted by being called Mers. The chief men are called Rao, and they have a multitude of Tikâis, of whom the principal are the Rao of Kukra and the Rao of Barâr" (*b*). The Râwats of Todgarh are exhibiting a strong tendency to adopt Brahminical usages

(*a*) Gazetteer of Ajmere-Merwara, by Mr. J. D. LaTouche, p. 35

(*b*) *Ibid.*

observed by neighbouring Rajpoots. Since 1874 they have refrained from eating the flesh of kine and buffaloes, and excommunicate those who do so.

The Chitas and Barârs intermarry, but never marry into their own tribes. Hindus marry Mahomedans, and Mahomedans, Hindus; the ceremony in both cases being performed by a Brahman, who leads the bride and bridegroom seven times round a fire. In some places the Mahomedan Merâts are beginning to adopt Mahomedan usages, and the Brahmanical marriage ceremony is being supplanted by one of an Islamitish character. In Merwara a large portion of the people are tending either to Brahmanism or Mahomedanism. The customs observed on the death of Chîta and Barâr women is curious. A Barâr woman married to a Chîta husband is buried at death; but, on the contrary, a Kâtât woman married to a Barâr husband, is burnt.

The social customs of the two tribes, however, are almost entirely similar. "A sonless widow retains possession of her husband's property till she marries again, or till her death." "Daughters do not inherit when there are sons alive." "All sons inherit equally." "There is no distinction between ancestral and acquired property." "A relation of any age may be adopted; the nearest relation has the first claim, and his children born before his adoption succeed in the adopted family." "Sons by slave girls, who are pretty numerous under the name of *dharmputr*, get land to cultivate, but obtain no share in the inheritance, and cannot transfer the land" (*a*).

II.—The Pramar Mair Tribe.

This tribe is also partly of Rajpoot origin. Both the Pramars and the Motîs are said to be descended from Dhârânâth Powar or Pramar, who built the city of Dharanagar, in Marwar, which, tradition says, was forty-eight miles in circumference. The Pramars were first settled at Rudhâna, to the south of Beawar, whence they spread over the surrounding country, establishing many villages, such as Biliawas, Jawaja, Bahâr, Barkochran, Rawat Mâl, Lusâni, and Akayjitgarh Naloi.

The Pramars are divided into six *gotras* or clans, namely :—

1. Delât. This is the largest of all the clans, and has possession of fourteen villages in Beawar and five in Todgarh. In Ajmere they occupy eleven villages, and have portions of eight others. They appear "to have pushed the other members of the tribe out of Merwara, who thereupon settled near Ajmere, and especially in the *purgannah* of Pushkar" (*b*).

(*a*) Gazetteer of Ajmere-Merwara, by Mr. J. D. LaTouche. p 36.
(*b*) *Ibid.*

2. Kallât. A small clan in possession of Kalâthân, in Beawar.

3. Doling. These possess Barla, Madarpura, and Gwari.

4. Boya. The villages of Hokran and Gudli belong to this clan.

5. Kheyat. Khwâjpura and Kana-khera are villages in their possession.

6. Pokhariya. These hold the villages of Pushkar, Ganahira, Naidla, and Naulakha.

The Pramars are an industrious people of finer stature than the Chauhân Mairs, whose customs they observe. They are commonly spoken of as Mairs, although they prefer to be addressed as Râwats. Their principal men are styled Gameti. Much social intercourse seems to prevail between them and the Chauhân Mairs, and they intermarry freely with Hindu Chitas and the Barârs. The Kâtâts of the Chîta tribe will not give their daughters in marriage to the Pramars; but will take Pramar women for their sons (*a*).

III.—The Motî Mair Tribe.

This tribe is descended from an ascetic, named Rohitas, of the family of Dhârânâth, and a Banjârâ woman, who lived together in a cave of the Mâkutji hill. After a time the woman separated from Rohitas, and she and her twin children resided under the roof of Khemchand, a Brahman of Bamunhera. A dispute arising between the boys and their protector, the Brahman expelled them from his house. One of them went to Marwar, the other continued in Bhaelan; and a deadly feud was carried on by his descendants and the Brahmans of the country on account of the treatment of their ancestor by Khemchand, the end of which was that, in the fifth generation, the Motîs. under their leader Makut, destroyed nearly the whole of the Brahmans, and seized the district of Bhaelan. The Mairs pay great respect to the memory of Makut, and worship him as a deity. A cow was yearly offered up in sacrifice at his shrine; and a fair is still held to his honour on the Mâkutji hill every September. The Motî Râwats, as they are called, possess fourteen villages in Bhaelan at the present day. They have estates also in Beawar and Ajmere (*b*).

IV.—The Dakul Mair Tribe.

These have sprung from the union of a Mina woman, of the Dakul Mina tribe, and a Brahman, who escaped from the general destruction of his race in Bhaelan, in the time of Makut, and fled to the village of Burar. He abandoned his caste, and became a Mair. The tribe is divided into several clans (*c*).

(*a*) Gazetteer of Ajmere-Merwara, by Mr. J. D. Latouche, pp. 36, 37.

(*b*) *Ibid*; and also Colonel Dixon's Mairwara, pp. 11, 12.

(*c*) Colonel Dixon's Mairwara, p. 12.

V.—*The Gahlot Mair Tribe.*

This tribe was founded by two Gahlot Rajpoots, who married two Mina women of Borwa, in Saroth, after the sack of Chitore by Ala-ud-din Ghori. They adopt the title of Râwat, and, notwithstanding their spurious descent, aspire to the dignity of pure Rajpoots, and style themselves Sûrajbansi Rajpoots. Their customs apparently are like those of other Mair tribes, and they intermarry with the Hindu Chaubân Mairs; but the Merâts, while receiving their women in marriage, will not reciprocate the favour by giving wives to Gahlot husbands. The tribe is split up into sixteen clans, the chief of which are the following:—

Gahlot Clans.

1. Godât.	5. Baniyât.
2. Medrat.	6. Lahr.
3. Kâchi.	7. Balot.
4. Pinga.	8. Dhâukal.

The Gahlots possess many villages in Merwara, and also Purbutpura, Ansari, Mayapur, Lakhshmipur, Borâj, and Amba Massena, in Ajmere (*a*). They have eleven villages in Beawar and Kukar Khera, in Todgarh.

VI.—*The Pataliyat Mair Tribe.*

These are descended from the Bhatti Rajpoots of Jesalmere, and are owners of the village of Baria Nagga.

VII.—*The Chaurot Mair Tribe.*

The Chaurots profess also to have sprung from the Bhatti Rajpoots of Jesalmere. They possess the village of Kalikankur Kishnpura. Some of the tribe have settled in Mohunpura, in Ajmere (*b*).

VIII.—*The Bharsal Mair Tribe.*

The Bharsals reside in the village of Ramkhera Dhanâr, and are located also in several villages in Ajmere.

IX.—*The Bûch Mair Tribe.*

These are found in Rajpur Bûchân, and likewise in two villages of Ajmere.

(*a*) Gazetteer of Ajmere-Merwara, by Mr. J. D. Latouche, p. 37.
(*b*) *Ibid.*

X.—*The Kharwal Mair Tribe.*

The headman of the town of Beawar is of this tribe, which inhabits Nayanagar and Fathpur.

XI.—*The Mamnot Mair Tribe.*

XII.—*The Selot Mair Tribe.*

XIII.—*The Banát Mair Tribe.*

XIV.—*The Banna Mair Tribe.*

These last tribes are scattered about a few villages.

CHAPTER VII.

SEC I.—THE JIT OR JAT TRIBE. SEC. II.—THE GUJAR TRIBES. SEC. III.—THE MEENA TRIBES. SEC. IV.—THE GRASSIA TRIBES. SEC. V.—THE BHEEL TRIBES.

Section I.—The Jit or Jât Tribe.

The Jâts were in possession of the north-western division of Rajputana before the Rajpoots entered the province, and there is good ground for believing that they had been there for a long period. Some persons have formed the idea that the Jâts are a branch of the Indo-Scythian from the banks of the Oxus.

Respecting the physical characteristics of the Jâts, Dr. Brereton makes the following remarks :—" In physique," he says, " the Jâts are generally of fair height, but below the average of Rajpoots or other castes. Their chest measurement and weight are in fair proportion to their height; the extremities, especially the lower, are often disproportionate to their abnormal length. The women are of very strong physique, exceeding the men in this respect, proportionately speaking. They are not remarkable for personal beauty, but some have very fine figures. They are also most industrious and contented, working in the fields, &c., but are said to rule their husbands. The prevailing complexion is fair, and the colour of the eyes, dark ; the hair is dark, fine, and straight ; beard and moustachios, scanty, and the former not usually worn. The crania are of tolerably fair size and shape, often elongated, altogether a lower type than the Brahman skull. Their intellectual faculties are not brilliant, partaking more of shrewdness and cunning than ability. They are said to possess courage and fidelity, are industrious and persevering in their habits, and are of an agile and muscular frame" (*a*).

This tribe commonly bears the name of Jit in Rajputana. In all the ancient lists of the Rajpoot tribes it is always placed among the thirty-six royal tribes. Now, however, in Rajputana it is never reckoned among them. The Jit and the Gûjars are the original cultivators of the soil in Ajmere-Merwara, and considerably outnumber every other tribe. Their chief possessions are in Ajmere, Tubeji, Suradhua, Makrera, Jethana, Budhwara, Pecholean, and the larger portion

(*a*) The Rajputana Gazetteer, Vol. I, p 162.

of the Ramsur *pargannah* belong to them: and they have settlements in Kekri and in some of the best villages of the Ajmere and Rajgarh *pargannahs.* The tribe in this tract is divided into three principal clans, namely:—

Jât Clans in Ajmere and Merwara.

1. Puniyo.	2. Seeshmo.	3. Harchitràl.

These clans have more than a hundred *gotras* or caste distinctions (*a*). They are hardworking, excellent cultivators, and are famous for their wells and their great diligence in improving their lands. None of them are *bhumias*, or occupy land free from revenue. They possess twice as much territory as the Gûjars, and pay three times more revenue. There were more than thirty thousand Jâts in Ajmere-Merwara in 1876. Their headmen are styled Chaudhri or Patel.

In Bikaneer there are, or were formerly, seven clans, as follows:—

Jât Clans in Bikaneer.

1. Godârâ	...	Their principal villages are	Ladhri and Shekhsar.
2. Lâran	...	Their principal village is	Bhâadang.
3. Kasvas	...	Ditto	Lidmûkh.
4. Beniwal	...	Ditto	Raisatâna.
5. Puniah	...	Ditto	Bara Lundi.
6. Sihaga	...	Ditto	Sûin.
7. Sodûan	...	Ditto	Dhansi (*b*).

The Godârâ Jâts place the *tikâ*, or sacred mark denoting rank or sovereignty, on the forehead of every successive ruling chief of the Bikaneer State.

The chief object venerated by the Jâts of Marwar, Ajmere, and Kishangarh is Teja Jî. This was a Jât who, according to a legend universally believed, lived some eight or nine hundred years ago, and was bitten in the tongue by a snake, which caused his death. The Jâts have the idea that if a man bitten by a snake tie a cord round his right foot, and repeat the words Teja Ji, he will recover (*c*). A fair is held at Kishangarh, in the month of July, in honour of Teja Jî, and he is worshipped in a temple erected to his memory at Sarsara. Most Jâts wear round their necks an amulet of silver representing Teja Jî on horseback, his sword drawn, and a snake in the act of biting his tongue.

At the marriage ceremony among the Jâts, a rupee and a cocoanut, emblems of wealth and fertility, are sent to the bride. A framework of wood, called *torun*,

(*a*) Gazetteer of Ajmere-Merwara, by Mr. J. D. Latouche, pp 30, 31.
(*b*) Gazetteer of the Bikanir States, by Captain Powlett, Political Agent, Ulwar, p. 4.
(*c*) Gazetteer of Ajmere-Merwara, p. 30.

is placed over the door of her house, and having been forcibly struck with a sword by the bridegroom when he approaches near, he enters within. This has been considered by some as a remnant of the custom of marriage by conquest (*a*). The marriage ceremony simply consists of the bride and bridegroom, under the direction of a Brahman, going round a fire lit in the centre of the room. The Jâts, as well as all the tribes of Merwara, permit the remarriage of widows. A man may marry the widow of his elder brother, not that of his younger brother. "In all castes, a widow who has no sons retains her deceased husband's property till her death or remarriage." The youngest brother has the first claim to marry the widow of a deceased brother. Widow-marriage is called Nâthâ. At marriages a sum of money is always paid for the wife, a custom which the women seem to like, as it in a fashion denotes their value. Marriages within the same *gotra*, or family order, are regarded as incestuous, and are forbidden.

The Jâts are numerous in the Bikaneer State, where their tribe is twice as large as any other. They are the agriculturists of that country; and are very heavily taxed for the lands they occupy. Before Bikaneer was conquered by Bika, the Jâts possessed the greater portion of the territory. Many are Vaishnavis, and will not take life. They will not even kill game, or sanction or help those who come to their fields for the purpose of doing so. This sect of the Jâts buries its dead.

This tribe had settled in Marwar long before the Râthors acquired possession of that State. Tod says, that in his time they constituted five-eighths of the population of Marwar.

The Jâts are excellent farmers in Mallâni, and have spread over the whole district. Members of this tribe are found throughout Rajputana, where they form the greater portion of the cultivating classes.

Several clans of the tribe are found in the Rajputana desert. Some of these are:

1. The Jakhurs.	2. The Shâghs.	3. The Pooniahs.

The Jâts of Jeypore are some of the principal landholders and cultivators in that State; and some of them have large estates. They have also, with the Gûjars, ten villages in Beawar. In Jeypore they are mostly in the north and west, and in the neighbourhood of the capital.

In the earlier part of the last century the Jâts of Bhurtpore made successful attacks on the Jeypore State, and were able to wrest therefrom a tract of country

(*a*) Gazetteer of Ajmere-Merwara, p. 39.

which was annexed to Bhurtpore. The founder of the State was Churaman, a Jât landholder, who, having erected two forts in the villages of Thun and Sinsiniwar, plundered the country in all directions, which, in spite of the efforts made to destroy him, he gradually gained possession of; and his family, through many vicissitudes, has retained its hold of it to the present day. In consequence of a disputed succession, Bhurtpore was besieged by British troops for six weeks, and was taken by storm by Lord Combermere on the 18th January, 1826.

The Jâts, Gûjars, and Ahirs of Bhurtpore smoke, and, under certain restrictions, eat together. Widows are sold indiscriminately to all three tribes. The Jâts of Bhurtpore number more than one hundred and twenty thousand persons, separated into numerous tribes, some of which are as follows :—

Jât Tribes of Bhurtpore.

1. Sinsiniwar.	4. Nohwar.	7. Aooe.
2. Khuntail.	5. Sogaiwar.	8. Naharwar.
3. Chahar.	6. Manga.	9. Pachandia.

10. Dâgur.

The first six tribes are highest in rank, and are known by the common designation of Dung. These have peculiar customs of their own. One is, that a Dung, on the death of his brother, does not take his widow to wife, as is the practice among the other tribes. The Jâts, generally, are not at all particular in the choice of a wife, and may take her from any tribe or caste. The Jât women are not secluded, with the single exception of the wives and daughters of chiefs and great landholders. The Jâts are polygamists. They are worshippers of Hindu deities, especially Krishna, and are, for the most part, Vaishnavites.

The head of the small State of Dholpore is a member of the Bamraulia family of Deswali Jâts, who traces his pedigree back to Jeth Singh, who, in the eleventh century, held lands in Bairat, to the south of Ulwar. Afterwards the family settled in Bamroli, and after many vicissitudes, in which it received the aid, first, of the Tonwâr Rajpoots, then of the emperors, next of the Mahrattas, and finally of the British, it found itself at the head of Dholpore, Bâri, and Rajakhera, by the treaty of 1805, having lost, however, Gwalior and Gohad, of which it was formerly possessed. The clan of the Rana, or chief, is divided into eight branches or families as under :—

1. Gadi (family of the chief).	3. Pachgaon.	6. Sur Kythoda.
2. Ekayuna.	4. Makoi.	7. Bhagwasi.
	5. Rajpura.	8. Dandrawa (a).

The clan next in importance in the State is that of Bidankria.

(a) The Rajputana Gazetteer, Vol. I. pp. 249, 250.

Section II.—The Gûjar Tribes.

The Gûjars have long been inhabitants of the tract of country to the north of the Arvalis, stretching on towards the Punjab and along the Jumna, from Bikaneer to Bhurtpore and Jeypore, where they are cultivators, horse-breeders, and herdsmen.

In stature they seem to be somewhat superior to the Jâts, whom they much resemble in social habits. Like them they eat animal food and drink spirits. In Bhurtpore their women do not labour in the fields.

These tribes occupy thirty-five villages in Ajmere, and also villages in the Meywar plain beyond. They are described as careless cultivators, devoting their chief energies to grazing cattle. Their principal deity is Deo Jî, a Gûjar who is supposed to have lived several hundred years ago, and to have worked miracles. Their customs are similar to those of the Jâts, with this important difference, however, that "property is divided according to wives, and not according to sons." The Gûjars and Jâts hold intimate social intercourse with one another, and will eat and drink together (*a*). The Chandela Gûjars are supposed to have settled among the hills surrounding Chang. The headmen of the Gûjars are styled Mihr.

The Gûjars are chiefly cultivators in Karauli, and are most numerous in the northern part of the State. In the south of Karauli Dâng they are the principal inhabitants, and bear a better character than their fellow clansmen of the Dholpore Dâng. Formerly, the Gûjars were notorious for cattle-lifting and stealing; but they have been led in many places to abandon these bad habits by the severe repressive measures which were adopted against them. The Gûjars are careless cultivators, and do not obtain such good crops as Jâts and Meenas (*b*). They are the proprietors of thirty-eight villages in Dholpore, while Gûjars are headmen of ninety-five more.

In Jeypore these tribes occupy an important position, and are in possession of extensive estates. They possess, with the Jâts, ten villages in Beawar. They chiefly occupy the southern and central districts of Jeypore, and are in the neighbourhood of Jhalrapatan.

The State of Bhurtpore contains nearly fifty thousand Gûjars, divided into two great branches—the Khari and Laur, each of which has a number of tribes.

(*a*) Gazetteer of Ajmere-Merwara, by Mr. J. D. Latouche, pp. 31, 32.

(*b*) Gazetteer of the Karauli State, by Captain P. W. Powlett. p. 19.

The Gújar Tribes of Bhurtpore.

The Laur Branch.

1. Kumhar.	3. Kisana.	5. Chadri.
2. Madi.	4. Sirande.	

The Khari Branch.

1. Solania.	3. Doralia.	5. Niskaria.
2. Thathwaria.	4. Sipwar.	6. Sua.
	7. Kharia.	

The Laurs occupy a higher social rank than the Kharis, with whom they neither eat nor intermarry. The Kharis are chiefly employed in making and selling butter.

Section III.—The Meena Tribes.

These tribes have played an important part in the history of Rajputana. In former times Rajpoot and Meena chiefs, in subordination to the Tuar kings of Delhi, ruled over a considerable tract of country. Towards the end of the tenth century, the Kachwâhâs dispossessed all of them from what is now the State of Jeypore. The Meenas are more or less connected with most of the tribes of Mairwara, and their clans are found scattered among the neighbouring States. But their character is not the same in all places. For example, in the north-east of Mewar and in Ajmere, the Meenas are a predatory, lawless people, with no settled habits, but passing their lives as robbers and dacoits. In this respect they resemble the Bheels of Rajputana, yet are more civilized than this wild race. They are numerous in the Jahazpore *pargannah*, in Mewar, whence they make their incursions. The agricultural Meenas of Karauli, on the contrary, are a quiet, orderly people.

The Meenas are said to be descended from those Rajpoots who, in the wars between their own tribes, or between them and the invading Mahomedans, were compelled to quit their native country, and to seek refuge in the fastnesses of Rajputana, where they formed alliances with aboriginal families, abandoned many of their caste usages, and established new tribes. It is not to be questioned that this singular people have sprung from unions between the Rajpoot immigrants and the aboriginal inhabitants of the country.

For the last four hundred years the Meenas have been the chief and most important cultivators in the Karauli State. They expelled the Dhangars and Lodhis, the dominant tribes in Karauli five hundred years ago, from a number of villages which they occupied, and have retained possession of them to the present time. These Meenas show their abhorrence of the infamous predatory practices of the Meenas of Kot Pûtti by refusing to intermarry with them. These disreputable Meenas were expelled from the Rajpoot villages of Inâiti Raontra, Sapotra, and Hadoti, where they had established themselves.

In Karauli, the three tribes of Gûjars, Meenas, and Jâts smoke together. "They eat together out of the same pot (degchi), but not out of the same dish (thâli). Their widows are sold to members of the caste, or even to a member of one of the other two. This is called 'daricha,' and is looked upon as an inferior sort of marriage, which gives the woman a position little better than a concubine or slave, but which legitimizes the children she may bear her master" (*a*). Some families of Meenas cultivate lands in Jhalawar.

Probably the Meenas were among the early inhabitants of Marwar. In Jeypore they occupy the highest positions of trust at the native courts. The Meena applies the mark of sovereignty to the forehead of every new chief, showing, says Tod, that the country was obtained from them originally by adoption rather than by conquest. In former times, that is, in the earlier stages of Kachwâhâ power, the Meenas "had the whole insignia of State, as well as the person of the prince, committed to their trust." They are among the principal cultivators of Jeypore, many possessing large estates. Some, however, are village watchmen and professional thieves.

The bards or minstrels of the Meenas are termed Dhâdî, Dholî, Dhom, and Jâegâ.

The tribes are divided into thirty-six sections, which are variously distributed. Some occupy the strongholds and fastnesses of the country, whither, doubtless; their ancestors were driven in earlier times to escape from the Rajpoot invaders. They are powerful in the northern portions of Jeypore and Ulwar, whence they proceed on their great plundering expeditions over Northern India. The tribe is scattered over all the north-eastern States on the banks of the Jumna. As many as twenty thousand are peaceable agriculturists in Bhurtpore and Dholpore, and a great many are employed in several States as village watchmen.

Although the tribes, as stated above, are generally regarded as consisting of thirty-six branches, yet in the Ulwar State it has one hundred and forty-six. The Meenas of Jeypore and Ulwar consider themselves as superior in rank to all other Meenas, and consequently will hold no intercourse with them. Some of them have a tradition that they are descended from an alliance between Brahman and Meena families.

(*a*) Gazetteer of the Karauli State, by Capt. P. W. Powlett, p. 19.

The Pârihar Meenas in the Bundee State and in the north-east of Meywar, were apparently in possession of this part of the country before the Rajpoots arrived, and gradually blended with the invaders. They have the character of being wild and daring plunderers. In the highlands of the country in the south-east of Meywar, in the direction of Neemuch, there are many small Meena villages inhabited by a marauding race. The lowest class of Meenas are those found in the desolate region to the north of Sirohee, occupying the Arvali hills, and being a constant torment to the neighbouring States. Other Meenas will neither eat nor drink nor intermarry with them (*a*).

The Meenas of Bhurtpore eat flesh, drink spirits, and are very superstitious. Their modes of worship are like those of Hindus, and, in taking an oath, they swear by the dagger. They pursue two occupations, and are either cultivators or village watchmen, the latter being prone to theft. The Bhurtpore Meenas are divided into the following tribes :—

The Meena Tribes of Bhurtpore (*b*).

1. Sanadan.	5. Gasika.	9. Bardar.
2. Jhardar.	6. Thorat.	10. Ghilot.
3. Lohara.	7. Bhokira.	11. Goadar.
4. Jordar.	8. Satkal.	

In the Bundee, Meywar, and Jeypore States the Pârihar Meenas inhabit a tract of country called Kerar, close to Deoli, extending for twelve miles from the town of Jahazpore eastwards. They claim to be descended from Shoma, son of Nahar Rao, ruler of Mundor, and a Meena woman. There is an inscription in the Kerar village, showing that they settled originally there in the twelfth century. Every village within a circuit of fifty miles has two or three families of this class of Meenas; but they do not intermarry with Meenas of other districts. The Pârihars adopt the Rajpoot custom of marrying members of clans other than their own. Consequently, as the remaining Meena tribes look down upon them, and refuse to hold social intercourse with them, the Pârihars find it a difficult matter sometimes to find husbands for their daughters, and wives for themselves.

The State of Dholpore has more than ten thousand Meenas, who are proprietors of thirteen villages, and cultivators of nearly twenty thousand acres of land. They are very old inhabitants of Bari and Baseri, and are most excellent landlords and cultivators. The tribe came originally, it is said, from Jeypore.

(*a*) The Rajputana Gazetteer, Vol. I, pp. 72, 73.
(*b*) *Ibid*, p. 163.

Section IV.—The Grassîa Tribes.

The Grassîas of Meywar are said to be descended from Chauhân Rajpoots, from Chainpareen, near Baroda, who were in the country before the Sisodias conquered Chittore. They have lost most of their Rajpoot habits, and are now a wild race associating closely with the aboriginal Bheels, whose daughters they take to wife, and living apart from more civilized people. "None of the Grassia chiefs have ever been subjugated by Meywar. They voluntarily proffered a nominal allegiance to the Ranas, and hence they hold the *bhûm*, or right of property in the land, over which the Rana has no power. They are not liable to be called on for regular service, to which they are not subject, or to attend at the capital; but they pay a small quit-rent in token of submission. The Bheels and Grassîas obey the orders of these rude chiefs, to whom they are devoted. Every endeavour to dispossess them has only resulted in failure; though it has been constantly attempted by the Ranas, who early conquered the valleys, but were effectually kept out of the hills, in which, however, they always found protection and shelter in times of difficulty" (*a*).

The wilderness of Bhakar, a desolate region of rugged hills, commencing to the south of Mount Aboo, is chiefly in the hands of the Grassîas. They are generally held to be somewhat higher in rank than the Bheels, with whom they associate freely.

The word 'Grassîa,' as used in Gujerat and Malwa, has a different signification from that which it bears in Rajputana. In the former provinces it is applied to the headmen of villages who have a prescriptive right to collect dues from travellers and also certain sums imposed on lands and roads. In Rajputana the word is "becoming applied to a separate set or group of persons associated, though it may be ordinarily taken to denote a halfblood between Bheel and Rajpoot"(*b*).

Section V.—The Bheel Tribes.

The Bheels are a wild, daring, outcast race scattered over Rajputana, of which they are regarded as the aborigines, although this supposition must be taken in a limited signification, inasmuch as in some parts traditions show that they are descendants of Rajpoots. It is exceedingly probable that, while some Bheel tribes have been formed from unions between Bheels and Rajpoots, others are altogether of pure aboriginal Bheel blood.

(*a*) History of Mewar, by Capt. J. C. Brookes, p. 3

(*b*) The Rajputana Gazetteer, Vol. I, p. 78.

The Bheel country may be said to commence in the north with the Arvali range. They are in greatest strength and most independent in the hills of the south-west of Meywar and Serohi, extending from Serohi to Dungarpore. Their villages are numerous among the forests and hills of Pertabgarh, Banswara, and Dungarpore, and in the Chappan, near Neemuch. There are said to be as many as two hundred thousand Bheels in the Meywar hills, divided into sixteen sub-tribes. Some small chiefs, such as those of Ogna, Panurwa, Jowra, and Jowas, regard themselves as of mixed Rajpoot and Bheel descent. In the wildest parts of the country "there are many powerful villages which own no immediate chief or master whatever, though they may be nominally subject to the State within whose territory they dwell. They live together in *pals*, which appear to be large settlements or collections of hamlets; for a Bheel village is not compact, but a scattered series of isolated huts. They usually follow the lead of some local headman or principal clansman. These *pals* in the small States of Dungarpore, Banswara, or Pertabgarh, are quite strong enough to defy the levies of the ruling chief. In these States, and in the Meywar hilly tracts, and to some degree in the Chappan, the Bheels have for many years given much trouble by their claim to levy blackmail throughout their country, and their inveterate habit of plundering; while it was difficult either to pursue the Bheel himself unto his fastnesses, or to fix the responsibility on the State to which he belonged territorially. The expeditions sent under British officers against the Bheels rarely effected anything permanent, while the native governments were only strong enough to oppress and exasperate without subduing them. In the course of time, however, matters have improved. The Bheels are now fairly pacified, and will be gradually reclaimed by careful management"(*a*).

The Bheel tribes are numerous, and it is much to be regretted that so little is known respecting them. The writers of works on Rajputana seem never to realize the interest connected with the individual tribes, not merely of the Bheels, but also of the other races inhabiting that tract of country; and content themselves, for the most part, with mere generalities and compendious statements. Each writer gives a few details on points which have arrested his attention, but not one, so far as my own acquaintance with their productions extends, has earnestly set himself the task of enquiring into separate clans and their subdivisions, and into their history, customs, manners, and distinctions.

Although the Bheels are not Hindus, yet they practise some of the rites of the Hindu religion. Their deities are chiefly local, they are very superstitious, and

(*a*) The Rajputana Gazetteer, Vol. I, pp. 75, 77.

have great faith in witchcraft. They do not appear to have any separate language of their own, but speak a peculiar Hindi dialect.

The Bheel tribes are sixty in number in Banswara, and are the most numerous of all the tribes of that State. Formerly, they had entire possession of this part of the country. At the present day the Bheel tribes have great power in the State, and are very jealous of the interference of the reigning prince in their affairs. In their villages, indeed, they utterly forbid such interference. They are a dirty race, and their women are small and ugly. The chiefs constantly wear swords, and all others always appear with their bows and arrows. They drink spirits, eat meat, and are passionately fond of quarrelling and fighting (*a*). The Bheel landholders exercise both civil and criminal jurisdiction over their lands.

These people live not so much in villages as in detached houses congregated together, "each built on separate hillocks at some distance from one another. The cultivation belonging to a family surrounds the homestead, and each congregation, or *pal*, thus covers a large extent of ground. This mode of living, by preventing surprise, gives the wild race greater security from the troops of the native States, who treat them rather as enemies than subjects. The jungle on the larger hills near the *pal* is allowed to grow; and, in case of attack, the Bheels flee into the cover with their families and cattle. Each homestead is complete in itself, consisting of several houses for grain and cattle within a single enclosure. Many of the Bheel houses in Meywar are well built, capacious, and tiled; and far superior to the habitations of the same class elsewhere. The Bheels lived originally in independent communities, each acknowledging its own leader. Those that were conquered by the Meywar sovereigns or chiefs, transferred their allegiance to them; whilst the greater portion, who coalesced with the Grassias, before the entry of the Udaipore family into the country, still remains faithful to these allodial or *bhûmia* chiefs" (*b*).

The Bheels and Grassias are much intermingled, the latter freely intermarrying with Bheel women. They obey, to some extent, the chiefs of the States in which they are settled; but the lands they occupy are their own, and no force has yet proved sufficiently strong to dispossess them.

The Bheels may be regarded as one of the aboriginal races of Marwar. They are found scattered about the Rajputana desert, where they are very degraded in their habits, even more so than the Kolis. They feed on foxes, jackals, rats,

(*a*) The Rajputana Gazetteer, Vol. I, p. 117.
(*b*) History of Mewar, by Capt. J. C. Brookes, p. 3.

guanas, snakes, and other vermin. Some Bheels are scattered about Ajmere, Merwara, and are addicted to thieving.

The tribe has some good cultivators in Mallâni, and also gives excellent servants to the chiefs. They form body-guards at marriage festivals, and are too prone to engage in village disputes.

One excellent custom in regard to marriage prevails among the Bheels in some districts. Girls are not betrothed in childhood, as is common among Hindus. Frequently it happens that a girl is not married until she is twenty or twenty-five years of age. The father of a girl can do nothing of himself to promote her marriage, but must wait, as in civilized countries, until a proposal is made on the part of a young man seeking a wife. When such a proposal is made, the question then comes, how much money is to be paid for the girl? (*a*).

The Bheels of Banswara erect stone tablets, with the figure of the deceased carved upon them, to the memory of their male dead. The figure is represented on horse-back, and sometimes on foot, with sword and shield, or a lance, in his hands. Deceased boys are honoured with tablets, on which a hooded snake is sculptured.

The principal inhabitants of the small State of Kusalgarh are Bheels. They have many clans also scattered about Dungarpore, of which State they are said to be the earliest or aboriginal inhabitants.

Respecting those tribes which are partly of Bheel and partly of Rajpoot descent, Sir John Malcolm remarks that they exhibit in their lives the defects of both, and are a proud, thievish, and debauched race. These Bhilalas, as they are termed, are, says Mr. Aberigh-Mackay, "descended from Rajpoots who have mingled their sacred blood with that of the abased people of the jungle They are half Rajpoot, half Bheel, but take the name of the Rajpoot clan to which they trace their origin. Nearly all the chiefs of the Bheel States on the Vindhyan slopes belong to this class. They affect to ignore their Bheel taint, and desire to be regarded as an ancient Rajpoot clan. But the forest lineage is deeply impressed on every line of their faces, and on every feature of their character"(*b*).

(*a*) The Rajputana Gazetteer, Vol. I, p. 118.

(*b*) The Chiefs of Central India, by Mr. G. R. Aberigh-Mackay, Vol. I, pp. xxxii, xxxiii.

CHAPTER VIII.

THE MAHOMEDAN TRIBES.

1.—SAIYID. 2.—KAIM-KHANI. 3.—KATAT MERAT. 4.—RATH. 5.—DAMMAMI. 6.—HAIWASI. 7.—PATHAN. 8.—DARAS. 9.—SAMEJA. 10.—SAMA. 11.—RAHAMA. 12.—NUHRI. 13.—ARISAR. 14.—MANGLIA. 15.—MALLAYA. 16.—BAKIYA. 17—JONIJA. 18.—HALIPOTRA. 19.—ABRA. 20.—BHAMSARA. 21.—MHER. 22.—CHAMA. 23.—JANJ. 24.—BHYA. 25.—SAUD. 26.—SANGRASI. 27.—KALLAR. 28.—CHICHAR. 29.—SAHTA. 30.—DAL. 31.—RAJAR. 32.—GAJJU. 33.—JHAKRA. 34.—THABA. 35.—RAMDAWA. 36.—BHATI. 37.—KATI. 38.—TALOZI. 39.—DEWAT. 40.—HINGORA. 41.—SARAI .42. DHANDAL. 43.—CHOPAN 44.—SUMRA. 45.—PANU. 46.—RIND. 47.—JESAR. 48.—SARWANI. 49.—LOWANI. 50.—KURURWANI. 51.—BAIDWANI. 52.—TOGRU. 53.—BRIKU. 54.—BARAHA. 55.—SEHRAE. 56.—KOSSA, OR KHOSSA. 57.—CHANDIA. 58.—SADANI. 59—SAMAICHA. 60.—OMAR. 61.—KALLORA. 62.—TALPURA. 63.—NUMRI, LUMRI, OR LUKA. 64.—MAIR, OR MER. 65.—MOHOR, OR MOR. 66.—TAWURI, THORI, OR TORI. 67.—JOHYA. 68.—DAHYA. 69.—BAIRAWI. 70.—KHAIRAWI. 71.—JANGRIA. 72.—UNDAR. 73.—BAGRIA. 74.—SHEIKH. 75.—AFGHAN. 76.—DESWALI. 77.—BANJARA. 78.—MEO. 79.—PIRADAS. 80.—RAHAT. 81.—MEWATTI. 82.—BOHRA.

Mahomedans are fewest in the States lying to the west and south-west, and perhaps fewest of all in Meywar. The influence of the great Moghul rulers of India in former times was powerfully felt in some parts of Rajputana, leading to the conversion to Islamism of many families connected with the Rajpoot tribes. The tribes situated nearest Delhi, such as those of Ulwar, Ajmere, and of the States bordering on the Jumna, were especially affected.

In Bhurtpore the Mahomedan population numbers one hundred and thirteen thousand persons, or eighteen per cent. of the entire community. Some hold high positions in the native court, while others are found in the army and police. They are in greatest numbers in the villages of Paharsar, Saidpura, Helak, and Rara. The Sunni sect preponderates greatly over the Shiah.

Many Mahomedans are found in Rajputana, especially in Ajmere and the eastern States, and not a few are in the employment of native chiefs. In Jesalmere one-third of the people are Mahomedans belonging to seventy-six tribes. In Merwara the Kâtât Merwâts, a degenerate class of Mahomedans, are numerous;

but in Bikaneer, Mahomedans form only a small community. The following classes of Mahomedans are scattered about the States of Rajputana:—

1. *Saiyids.*

In Bikaneer there are many Saiyid sepoys. In Karauli the Saiyids have a mosque, and hold various offices of respectability. There are more than three thousand Saiyids in Ajmere. There are some also in Bundee and other States.

2. *Kâim-Khâni.*

In Bikaneer, Mahomedans descended from Chauhân Rajpoots. They are settled about Futtehpoor Jhoon-joonee, and form a numerous class in Shekhawati. These last were originally Chauhân Rajpoots, and are said to have once possessed the Shekhawati District, but were dispossessed by Sheikh Jî, the founder of the Shekhawat tribe. The ancestors of the Kâim-Khânis were Rajpoots, who fought against Baber in 1528

3. *Kâtât Merât.*

Degenerate Mahomedans of Merwara. They are intimately associated with the Hindu Mer tribes, from whom they originally sprang. Until lately the Mers and Merâts intermarried.

4. *Râth.*

Mahomedans in Bikaneer of Rajpoot extraction. They belong to four clans, two descended from Chauhâns, one from Tuars, and one from Saroas.

5. *Dammâmî.*

Mahomedan kettledrum-beaters in Bikaneer.

6. *Haiwâsî.*

Converts from the Haiwâsî Brahmans of Marwar.

7. *Pathâns.*

Pathâns are the most important Mahomedans in Karauli, and are regarded as the most trustworthy of the troops of the durbar. There are a few in Ajmere and Bundee.

8. *Daras.*

In Mallâni.

9. *Sameja.*

In Mallâni.

10. *Samá.*

In Mallâni.

11. *Râhamâ.*

In Mallâni.

12. *Nuhri.*

In Mallâni.

13. *Arisar.*

In Mallâni.

14. *Manglia.*

In Mallâni and the Rajputana desert. Rajpoot proselytes to Islam.

15. *Mallaya.*
In Mallâni.
16. *Bakiya.*
In Mallâni.
17. *Jonijá.*
In Mallâni.
18. *Hálipotra.*
In Mallâni.
19. *Abra.*
In Mallâni.
20. *Bhamsara.*
In Mallâni.
21. *Mher.*
In Mallâni.
22. *Châma.*
In Mallâni.

23. *Janj.*
In Mallâni.
24. *Bhyâ.*
In Mallâni.
25. *Sâud.*
In Mallâni.
26. *Sangrâsi.*
In Mallâni.
27. *Kallar.*
In Mallâni.
28. *Chichar.*
In Mallâni.
29. *Sahta.*
In Mallâni.
30. *Dal.*
In Mallâni.

31. *Râjar.*

In Mallâni, the Rajputana desert, and the borders of Jesalmere ; they are said to be descended from the Bhâtî Rajpoots. They are, says Tod, "cultivators, shepherds, and thieves, and are esteemed the very worst of the converts to Mahomedanism."

32. *Gajju.*
In Mallâni.
33. *Jhakrâ.*
In Mallâni.

34. *Thâbâ.*
In Mallâni.
35. *Râmdawa.*
In Mallâni.

36. *Bhâti.*

In Mallâni and Bikaneer ; converts from Hinduism.

37. *Kati.*
In Mallâni.
38. *Tâlozi.*
In Mallâni.
39. *Dewat.*
In Mallâni.

40. *Hingora.*
In Mallâni.
41. *Sarai.*
In Mallâni.
42. *Dhândal.*
In Mallâni.

43. *Chopân.*
In Mallâni.

44. *Sumrâ.*

In Mallâni and the Rajputana desert, they are converts from the Pramara Rajpoots.

45. *Panu.*	46. *Rind.*	47. *Jesar.*
In Mallâni.	In Mallâni.	In Mallâni.

The Mahomedans of Jesalmere are divided into seventy-six classes or clans.

48. *Sarwâni.*

A branch of the Chauhân Rajpoots, settled in Shekhawati.

49. *Lowâni.*

A branch of the Chauhân Rajpoots, in Shekhawati.

50. *Kururwâni.*

A branch of the Chauhân Rajpoots, in Shekhawati.

51. *Baidwâni.*

A branch of the Chauhân Rajpoots, in Shekhawati.

52. *Togru.*

A branch of the Solankhî Rajpoots, in the Punjnud.

53. *Briku.*

A branch of the Solankhî Rajpoots, in the Punjnud.

54. *Baraha.*

A tribe of Rajpoot converts to Islam in the Raputana desert.

55. *Sehrâe.*

One of the most numerous of the tribes in the Rajputana desert. They are notorious robbers, and are the terror of that wilderness.

56. *Kossa, or Khossa.*

A branch of the Sehrâes, with similar habits.

57. *Chandia.*

A branch of the Sehrâes.

58. *Sadani.*

A branch of the Sehrâes.

These Sehrâe tribes are chiefly found in the southern part of the desert, about Noakote, Mittie, to Buliari. Formerly, they were very notorious for their depredations.

59. *Samaicha.*

Proselytes to Islam from the Soda Rajpoots, inhabiting the Rajputana deserts. Tod observes respecting them, "that they never shave or touch the hair of their heads. and consequently look more like brutes than human beings. They allow no animal to die of disease, but kill it when they think there are no hopes of recovery. The Samaicha women have the reputation of being great scolds, and never veil their faces" (*a*).

60. *Omar.*

A branch of the Pranava Rajpoots, in the Rajputana desert.

61. *Kallora.*

A Belooch tribe, in the lower part of the Rajputana desert. See the chapter on the Scinde tribes.

62. *Tâlpura.*

A Belooch tribe, in the lower part of the Rajputana desert. See the chapter on the Scinde tribes.

63. *Nûmrî or Lûmrî, or Lûka.*

A Belooch tribe, in the lower part of the Rajputana desert. See the chapter on the Scinde tribes.

64. *Mair, or Mer.*

A branch of the Bhâtî Rajpoots, in the lower part of the Rajputana desert.

65. *Mohor, or Mor.*

A branch of the Bhâtî Rajpoots, in the lower part of the Rajputana desert.

66. *Tawuri, Thori, or Tori.*

On this tribe Tod has the following remarks: "These engross the distinctive epithet of *bhût*, or evil spirits, and the yet more emphatic title of 'sons of the devil.' Their origin is doubtful, but they rank with the Bawurîs, Khengârs, and other professional thieves scattered over Rajputana, who will bring you either your enemy's head, or the turban from it. They are found in the Thuls of Dâûdputra, Beejnote, Noke, Noakote, and Udar. They are proprietors of camels, which they hire out, and also find employment as convoys to caravans" (*b*).

67. *Johya.*

Rajpoot proselytes to Islam, in the lower part of the Rajputana desert.

68. *Dahya.*

Rajpoot proselytes to Islam, in the Rajputana desert.

69. *Bairawi.*

A Belooch tribe, in the Rajputana desert.

(*a*) Tod's Rajasthan—Madras Edition—Vol. II, p. 294.
(*b*) *Ibid*, p. 295.

70. *Khairawi.*

Rajpoot proselytes to Islam, in the Rajputana desert.

71. *Jungria.*

Rajpoot proselytes to Islam, in the Rajputana desert.

72. *Undar.*

Rajpoot proselytes to Islam, in the Rajputana desert.

73. *Bagria.*

Rajpoot proselytes to Islam, in the Rajputana desert.

74. *Sheikh.*

There are upwards of three thousand Sheikhs in Ajmere-Merwara. The Sheikhs are found in several States.

75. *Afghan.*

Upwards of seven thousand Afghans are resident in Ajmere-Merwara.

76. *Deswâli.*

Rajpoots converted to Mahomedanism. They hold two villages in the north of Ajmere. The tradition is, that their ancestors changed their faith in the reign of Shahâb-ud-dîn.

77. *Banjâra.*

Converted to Mahomedanism, it is stated, at the same time as the Deswâlis. There are some in Ghegul.

78. *Meo.*

An indigenous tribe, converted to the Mahomedan faith, inhabiting Ulwar and Bhurtpore in large numbers. They retain, however, a good many Hindu religious customs. While they make pilgrimage to tombs of Mahomedan saints, they, at the same time, observe the Hindu idolatrous festivals of the Holi and Diwâli. Like the Rajpoots, the members of one clan do not intermarry, but marriages are invariably contracted between members of different tribes. They intermarried with Meena families until lately. The names of some of the Meena and Meo clans are the same. The Meos are now an agricultural people.

The chief territory in the occupation of the Meos is called Mewat, and lies partly in Bhurtpore, partly in Ulwar, and partly in lands under British jurisdiction. It is one hundred miles from north to south, and eighty from east to west. They are divided into twelve *pâls* or clans, some of which are as follows:—

Meo Clans.

1. Singal.	4. Doudolote.	7. Ratawat.
2. Nae.	5. Chirglote.	8. Darrawal.
3. Doolote.	6. Sundawat.	9. Khosa.

79. *Pîradâs.*

Descendants of a Mahomedan saint, occupying the lands between Anupgurh, Pugal, and Marot, in Bikaneer.

80. *Rahat.*

A small tribe of converts to Islam in Bikaneer.

81. *Mewâtti.*

These Mahomedans are found in the State of Bundee.

82. *Bohra.*

A small community of traders in Bundee.